I'm privileged to share my book *Heaven Within You! Cures for the Ailing Soul* with you. It contains a collection of heartfelt musings, poems and parables intended to shed light on the beauty of life within and around us. With each word, my intention is to stir emotions by brining to light **a wide range of circumstances** that we have all found ourselves in at one point or another. On these pages, you'll find passages on wisdom, kindness, decency, optimism, marriage, parenting, disappointment, faith and common sense.

In addition to being an author, I'm a doctor of internal medicine and a medical lecturer in Sibiu, Romania, and I sprinkle that expertise throughout *Heaven Within You*.

I've also written articles for Catchy.ro, a website with 150,000 Facebook followers, and Bel-Esprit, an online review. I'm confident that you'll enjoy the English version of *Heaven Within You* as much as my thousands of European fans have enjoyed the Romanian version.

With great sincerity,

Dan Orga-Dumitriu

HEAVEN WITHIN YOU!
Cures for the Ailing Soul

by

Dr. Dan Orga-Dumitriu, MD, PhD

New York

2019

VIRGO
ebooks

The scanning, uploading and distribution of this book via the Internet or via any other means without the permission of the publisher is illegal and punishable by the law. Please purchase only authorized copies and do not participate in or encourage electronic piracy of copyrighted materials.

The author appreciates your support.

Crowdfunding campaign - recognized as:

Angel (500 USD contribution):
Laura and Valeriu Roman
Robert Blaj

Patron (300 USD contribution):
Albert Ioo
Pr. Cosmin Antonescu
Nicolae Uca

Producer (160 USD contribution):
Cosmin Balcu
Cornel Benchia
Mircea Colceriu
Pr. Mircea Vasiu

Sponsor (100 USD contribution):
Stefan Giurgiu
Tiberiu Dragan
Gabriel Tischer
Adrian Dragoman
Dumitru Puiu
Adriana and Gabriel Moldovan
Renate Mueller-Nica
Ramona Tiepac
Valerica Nicu
Mircea Patac
Ianina Roberts
Alexandra and Liciniu Lupu-Petria
Andrei Mihu
Pr. Karol Bratosin
Pr. Marius Dumitrescu
Mariana Dogaru

Special thanks to:

Metropolitan Nicolae of the Romanian Orthodox
Metropolia of the Americas

Cosmin Balcu

Cornel Benchia

Adrian Dragoman

Raul Folea

Albert Ioo

Alexandra Iordache

Tom S. Johnson

Mother Superior Veronica from Alba Iulia

Valerica Nicu

Pr. Cosmin Antonescu

Pr. Prof. Theodor Damian

Pr. Prof. Aurel Pavel

Dumitru Puiu

James Rector

Mariana Terra

Andra Tischer-Podia

Foreword

"The book *Heaven Within You! Cures for the Ailing Soul* by Dr. Dan Orga-Dumitriu is an invitation to a deep reflection on our life, with its joys and sorrows, with the light rays of happy moments and the shadows of the states of helplessness. The author himself says it is a "collection of known or less known, but wonderful parables, poems and maxims" assembled with the intention of offering a "symphony of emotions".

I found in the pages of this book a beautiful explanation of the parable of the talents of St. Matthew Gospel (25, 14-30): the two servants who received five, respectively two talents and valued them, have received the same reward: the entrance to the master's joy. If we multiply the gifts received from God we will have a fulfilled life. We must not compare our gifts with those of our fellow men, we must not covet more or wish less. The fulfillment is the same because we turn the gifts to the Giver, we have a life full of this dialogue with God the Giver.

Through many parables and maxims the author of this book actually teaches us this fundamental lesson of human life: the joy of working together with God. We find this joy in ourselves and around us. In this order, we can fulfill the exhortation of the book – Heaven could be what you've already had!

We congratulate the author and we warmly recommend this book to those who wish to make a heartfelt reading!"

† Metropolitan Nicolae
of the Romanian Orthodox Metropolia of the Americas

i

Review by Andra Tischer-Podia

Below, you'll find a review of *Heaven Within You* by Andra Tischer-Podia. She is an editor and writer at *Catchy.ro* and the creative director of *Bel-Esprit*, an online magazine. She's also the author of *Unwritten Laws*, a published poetry collection, and a teacher of Romanian language at Octavian Goga National College in Sibiu. Ms. Tischer-Podia has had important collaborations within The Literary Circle in Cluj, and she annually organizes The National Contest of Literature and Arts Creation, Literary Critique, and Translations.

"More than anything, I wanted to give the world all the positive energy that fills my life. And at the same time, I longed to awaken emotions that expose circumstances that all of us are familiar with." The author wrote these words on the first page of his book *Heaven Within You*. They situate him between two fascinating worlds that connect to each other by invisible threads.

Both medicine (his professional calling) and a passion for writing (his inner calling) allow his spirit to travel beyond the limits of the human body. Thus, we can almost imagine his words as belonging to Vasile Voiculescu, who dedicated his life to attending to the wounded during the first World War while he wrote similar pieces of literature.

Hence, this book is not only aimed at bringing forth (a very lucid and sincere) *anatomy* of the reality of our times. But as the writer himself declares, it's also intended to create a "symphony of emotions" that's able to become a cure for ailing souls.

In a world set on *fast-forward*—always on the run, full of prejudgment—the doctor discovers his blessed gift of *soul therapy*, which he chooses to turn into a responsibility to people in need: "Sometimes, you will discover the sadness of the violin notes, meant to fill your eyes with drops of fresh morning dew and light. Other times, your soul will be filled with the joyful sound of a piano caressing your soul or the delicate touch of a harp touching your heart. And sometimes, the penetrating notes of a cello will give you the deepest sensations of life's cruel ways."

It's important for readers to remain aware of the intricacies of this particular book. This piece is not a common one, but a book of life and wisdom. First and foremost, you have to prepare yourself for a great performance in which *emotions* play the most important and difficult role (second only to the people conveying them.)

Let's call the scene they perform Heaven, disregarding the interference of religious precepts. In this scene, the soul in and of itself—the writer's soul—addresses each and every part of the audience members attending the great show of Life.

As a writer, Dr. Dan Orga-Dumitriu doesn't overlook the main values that play other important roles in the structure of the human personality: love, friendship, empathy, solidarity, generosity, and aspiration. Starting with the first lines of the book, these values become the steps of a pyramid of initiation into life, which offer ways to access the promised Heaven.

Today, the world is devoured by the pursuit of material fulfillment, devalued by the expiration of authentic values, and virtually accessible by a click. Since this accessibility is taking the place of authentic human relations, it's building more and more walls between people—annihilating the goodness, the beauty, the purity. But Dan Orga-Dumitriu's book opens the way to the spirit through love and art.

As a value, trust must be earned. It starts with one's own value system, and it must gradually be built (or recovered, if we think in ancestral terms) through positive thinking and love. Trust provides the great gift of restoring the connections between people. Thus, it can renew friendship, sincerity, and faith. All of these qualities will be able to (re)construct Paradise in its ethereal form of unconditional love.

While this undertaking certainly isn't easy, this clearly gifted author strongly believes in the power of the mind and soul. This balance allows this book to not only be a delight for readers, but also a source of authentic emotion. And most importantly, it's a book of wisdom that can be passed on to those who will follow.

Thus, to be a successful handbook for life, it consistently embodies the three purposes of literature: *docere, movere, delectare* (in the original Latin). In other words, it aims at spreading the Light that we definitively need.

Descending from Heaven, we keep on bearing parts of it within us, as long as we live, sometimes without being aware of the treasure we have been blessed with. But somewhere along the way, there is a moment when we realize that we need to go deeper into ourselves because there is a light that shines from the inner depths, making its way to the surface—to the conscience that guides us spiritually and gives us hope and a reason to be alive. There is no greater self-accomplishment than discovering one's inner force, no matter how hard the way or how late the moment.

Beyond a shadow of a doubt, Dan Orga-Dumitriu's book *Heaven Within You* **succeeds at opening a door to the special place within our souls that is truly authentic**. After walking through this door, we begin an intimate search to the parts of Heaven we miss in order to regain wholeness.

Every short story contained in this book is part of a recipe for the values that mankind holds most sacred—love, respect, friendship, success, compassion, and generosity. But it is also a guide to overcoming the difficult moments we come across during this journey called 'life.' In a world of hatred and pain, rancor and suffering, more and more affected by the cruel and fast evolution of technology that tend to annihilate human relationships, confusion takes over—digging more and more into the conscience and building walls between people, instead of authentically connecting them, by means of the soul. Tragedies happen because humanity no longer recognizes the Good and the Truth, and the Light of Wisdom from the bleakness of uncertainty.

And here is this book, which brings forth the need to regain stability, decency, harmony within oneself and furthermore, within the individuals composing the huge collective we live in. By means of storytelling, it recompounds the image of a world built on the principles of Beauty and Good (kalokagathia), as in the great books of wisdom belonging to those ancient times. The one who tells all these stories is not merely a storyteller, but a spiritual guide, a master fully invested with sacred powers to enlighten those who want to listen to his words.

The stories in *Heaven Within You* are allegories— short and penetrating—with common sense and true-to-life characters that are really intended to bring the values of the ideal world, as initially created by God, into the reader's conscience. Finding Heaven Within, Improving Yourself, and Building Healthy Relationships are not only parts of a book, but also steps to regaining confidence and well-being, as well as contributing to a better society through love and understanding.

One can read it as a book of leisure, but also as a book of wisdom, without it losing its attractiveness. *Heaven Within You* should be a **must read** for everyone.

Table of Contents

To my wife Gina
and the two wonders in our lives,
Ruxandra and Georgia

Introduction

"We build too many walls and not enough bridges."
Isaac Newton

"Two brothers lived in a village. As it often happens among siblings, one day they had a fight and exchanged harsh words. However, unlike after a simple sibling rivalry, they no longer spoke to each other after that.

Then one morning, someone knocked on the elder brother's door. He opened the door and saw a man. 'I beg your pardon,' the stranger said. 'I'm a woodworker, looking for a job. Do you happen to have one for me?'

'Actually, I do,' the elder brother answered. 'See my neighbor's house across the river? He's also my brother. I'm terribly upset with him, and I never want to see him again! So by the time I return from the field this evening, please build me a fence three meters tall.'

The elder brother left for work, and the carpenter started doing what he did best: he made measurements, cut the wood, and hammered in nails. When the elder brother came home that evening, he was dumbfounded. Instead of the fence he requested, the carpenter had built a bridge five meters wide and seven meters long, which the younger brother was crossing at that very moment.

Deeply moved, the younger brother exclaimed, 'I cannot believe you made this grand gesture after all the harsh words I said to you. You are a wonderful man, brother. Please forgive me!' They hugged and made up.

Meanwhile, the carpenter gathered his tools and prepared to leave. But the elder brother stopped him and said, 'Please stay for a few more days, as I have more work for you!'

The carpenter replied: 'I'm sorry, but I cannot stay any longer. I have other bridges to build... ' "

One of my friends sent me this story few years ago. I still share it with those dear to me, and I pass it on to every generation of students which I shepherd in for medical internships. I advise them to build bridges between themselves and those around them. The "building supplies" can be anything beautiful in their lives – a parable, a poem, a song, a thought or an emotion.

Choosing Love

After relaying this parable at a meeting for my interns, one of them replied by telling me another extraordinary tale:

"While changing a tire on a brand-new car, a man saw his seven-year-old boy scratching the hubcap with a nail. Losing his temper, the man hit the little boy on his fingers, not realizing he was still holding the tire iron.

Due to bone fractures, the little boy was rushed to the hospital, where he had to have his fingers amputated. Upon seeing his father, the boy's innocent eyes welled up with tears, and he asked, 'Daddy, will my fingers grow back?'

Devastated with guilt, the man went down to the parking lot, and hit the car with the tire iron several times! Then he saw the boy's scrawl and froze. It said: 'DADDY, I LOVE YOU!'

So this parable also ends with a wise moral: love and anger are boundless. If you want to have a good life, choose the former. People were made to be loved, and things like cars were meant to be used. But too often today, people are used, and things are cherished."

A Symphony for the Soul

For 20 years, I have worked with patients in distress. Beyond the already present wariness that occurs when interacting with a stranger, trauma tends to put an additional burden on the way a patient relates to a doctor. My mentor, Dr. Radu Ciuchendea, used to say, "It's an art, but also a necessity to know how to approach the patient. You must begin with the healing of the spirit to initiate the healing of the body, because disease first bites from the spirit!"

I followed his advice, and after years of practicing empathy and developing my bedside manner, thousands of patients have expressed their gratitude. One of them pleased me with this unforgettable metaphor (and it doesn't translate too well verbatim, but the point will come across): "Well, you are such a doctor that I could drink water from your mouth!" Because my mouth had turned into a spring, I realized that there are many people to nourish, so the idea of a book naturally emerged.

So here's the gift you'll find inside this book: a collection of known or less known, but wonderful musings, poems and parables that have given birth to many analyses and personal comments, in order to reveal the good side of being human. I have experienced far too many beautiful moments in life, so it would be a shame not to share them with other people.

The following pages contain insights that will perfectly match many circumstances in your own life – I have no doubt about that. These musings might even change your attitudes for the better because they act like common-sense pills that heal us when we're most vulnerable. In the end, all I want is for my readers to open up emotionally by revisiting various situations we've all encountered at different points in our lives.

I am convinced that you will enjoy this book as a symphony of emotions. Sometimes, you'll discover the sad sound of violins that makes you cry. Other times, you'll feel the joyful sound of a piano that makes your soul laugh, or the delicate sound of a harp that touches your heart. And sometimes, the mournful sound of a cello will remind you of how cruel life can be. An overwhelming number of readers of the Romanian edition said it spoke to their souls – and I hope you can share that same experience, dear reader!

Blinded by Burdens

We all have burdens that we must carry during our journey here on Earth, and we all have trials along the way. However, when we miss the true value of humanity because of these hardships, we also lose our way – and potentially ourselves – instead of finding a way to our *heaven within*.

Sometimes, our burdens will be light, and other times, they will be heavy. Sometimes, they will only last for a short period of time, but other times, they will go on for what seems like lifetimes. But if we make sure our souls and spirits keep their eyes on the Greatness of God, it will be much easier for us to accomplish our goals in life.

Heaven is so close to each of us! We find it in everything we do when we focus on love, kindness, decency, understanding, and compassion for the people around us – and we find it every time we touch their souls.

What a wonderful gift God has bestowed upon us by breathing life into clay! Far too often, we don't realize or fully appreciate how lucky we are to be alive. *Why?* It's obvious: Life's trials and tribulations distract us from the many beautiful things around us. Caught up in a storm of all-encompassing stimuli, we become too busy, proving Parkinson's Principle that "life is a continuous movement." And the consequences are that we spend way too little time enjoying its miracles.

To experience more, one must first reach inward, through mindfulness and contemplation, then learn to break away from the tumult of day-to-day life.

The Black Dot

A renowned American psychologist once talked at a conference. He showed his audience a piece of paper with a large black dot in the center. He then asked them what he was holding. Most of the audience replied, "A black dot." Only a few people said he was holding a piece of paper with a black dot in the middle. The psychologist then made a brilliant point that we often relate to life in the same way. Instead of seeing the many reasons why we should be grateful to God, we'd rather focus on the black dot— the embodiment of our discontent, the one thing that feeds us with negativity instead of fulfillment, the black cloud looming over the piece of heaven that resides within us.

The title of the book means that all you need throughout your life is already inside you! You don't have to look for what you need outside, because it's already there within you, and if you know that, then you can achieve everything you want by starting from there. It's not just a mindset; starting at birth, we truly carry a piece of divine energy with us—the heaven that God has breathed into us.

I don't intend to give you a step-by-step guide on how to live your life. I've learned that there isn't one single path to happiness; rather, the path itself brings happiness, and my path may differ from yours.

Yet, inside this book, you'll find principles and tactics for acting and reacting in various circumstances, so you can find your way along the path of your spiritual evolution. My intention with this book is to give the world something beautiful and meaningful to brighten spirits and warm souls, as these are the essential conditions for the heaven within each of us to reveal itself – and I hope you find that is the case! So be it!

Part I:
Finding Heaven Within

Chapter 1: Prejudices

"You know what I've done, but you don't know what I've been through."
Romanian Expression

"On the first day of school, Ms. Thompson lied to her 5th grade students, like most teachers do: She told them she loved them all the same. But that statement didn't hold true regarding one little boy named Teddy Stallard, who sat in the first row. She noticed several things about him. First, the boy didn't play with the other kids. His clothes were unkempt and dirty most of the time. He was generally unbearable, and it got to the point that Ms. Thompson enjoyed marking his papers with large red Xs and failing him.

At the end of the first quarter, Ms. Thompson reviewed all the students' records. She intentionally left Teddy's for last. When she opened his file, she was surprised to read what his 1st grade teacher had written: 'Teddy is a smart child. He does his homework neatly. He has good manners, and it's a pleasure to have him around.' His story evolved with each report card. His 2nd grade teacher wrote: 'Teddy is an excellent student. He is well-appreciated by his colleagues, but he is troubled by the fact that his mother is suffering from an incurable disease. Life at home must be really difficult.' His 3rd grade teacher mentioned: 'His mother's death has been hard on him. He's struggling, and his father doesn't show much interest in him. If nothing changes, his home life will soon affect him.' Teddy's 4th grade teacher concluded: 'Teddy is withdrawn and has lost interest in school. He doesn't have many friends, and he sometimes sleeps in class.'

Now that Ms. Thompson finally understood the boy's problem, she was ashamed of what she'd done. She felt even worse when the students brought her Christmas gifts wrapped in beautiful ribbons and bright paper – except for Teddy, whose present was wrapped in brown paper. Some of the students started laughing when Ms. Thompson took out a bracelet with some jewels missing and a half-empty perfume bottle. But she told the students that the bracelet was pretty, and the perfume smelled nice. Teddy waited after school to tell her, with tears in his eyes 'Ms. Thompson, you smell just like my mum now!'

After all the children were gone, Ms. Thompson cried for almost an hour. Then she started teaching her students more than just the curriculum; she started teaching them about life.

Ms. Thompson paid particular attention to Teddy. The more she encouraged him, the more his mind opened up. By the end of the year, he was once more the smartest child in class, and despite her promise that she would love them all the same, Teddy became her favorite.

A year later, she received a letter from Teddy, telling her she was the best teacher he'd ever had in his entire life. Two years later, she received another letter, which revealed he'd been admitted to a prestigious secondary school. Then four years later, she received yet another letter, saying he was the salutatorian of his senior class, and reiterated she was still the best teacher he'd ever had.

Four years later, she received another letter, saying he was about to graduate from college with an excellent GPA. In this letter, he reemphasized that she was still the best teacher. After some time, another letter arrived with the same message, but the sender's name had slightly changed: Theodore Stallard, MD.

Then a letter arrived saying that the young doctor was about to get married, but that his father had died. He asked if she would like to come to his wedding and sit in the place reserved for the groom's mother. Of course, she accepted. She wore the bracelet, the one that was missing some jewels, and she put on the same perfume he'd given her so long ago.

They hugged, and Teddy whispered in her ear, 'Thank you for believing in me. Thank you for making me feel important and for showing me that I could make a difference. 'Tears welling up in her eyes, Ms. Thompson whispered back, 'Teddy, you've got it all wrong. You were the real teacher, the one who taught me that I hold the power to change people. I didn't know how to teach children until I met you!'

So, remember, you never know what difference you could make in somebody's life by what you do or don't do. Keep this moral in mind as you travel through life and try to change the lives of others for the better. No one has the right to look down on anybody, unless they are bending down to help them get back on their feet."

As a physician, I have had many moments when I saw Teddy in the eyes of some patients on whom time and disease had left their mark. Some of them were brought to the hospital from nursing homes because no one was around to care for them: either their children lived far away, or they didn't have relatives to help them. I met them on hospital beds, often dressed in shabby pajamas and hiding behind beards because their tremoring hands could no longer shave without cutting their faces. They looked as if they were caught between two worlds: one that wouldn't let them go yet and another that wasn't ready to take them.

As I interacted with these men and women, I often found out that they'd commanded the respect of others and contributed to their communities throughout their lives. In fact, they'd earned respect due to their educations and positions, but their lights had faded due to the ravages of disease. They may have proudly travelled the world in their prime, as celebrated as *The Titanic*. But just like that doomed ship, there was no way to predict they'd end up being the human wreckage that sat before me.

Therefore, let's refrain from judging a book by its cover. Likewise, let's stop judging a person by the chapter during which we enter his life since we have not read his entire book. And most important, the book about one's life is still being written!

The Two Apples

"A little girl was holding two apples in her hands. With a smile on her face, her mother gently asked her, 'Dear, will you give me one?' The girl looked at her for a few seconds. Suddenly, she took a bite from one apple, then the other. The girl's gesture was so unexpected that her mother's smile froze on her face. She was making a huge effort not to reveal her disappointment when the girl handed over one of the bitten apples and said, 'Here you go, mum! This one is sweeter!' "

Whether we're aware of it or not, most people are more concerned about judging others than helping them. Oftentimes the best approach is to remind ourselves that we are all God's creations. And so we pay the price for having sinned: instead of loving one another, we end up hating each other. Instead of rewarding good, we prefer to do harm. Instead of appreciating one another, we savor others' suffering.

How many times have we acted as judges and made final decisions, without hearing the necessary perspectives? We do this because we're convinced by what we see or hear. More than once, I've wrongly labeled an individual, based on incomplete information. But eventually, I learned that when someone I know does something out of character, I should give them a chance to explain themselves. Their explanations have sometimes proven to be justified to the point that it did not change my opinion of them.

Nevertheless, we may not be able to stop ourselves from judging other people. Up to a certain point, this reaction is normal. After all, we are just as prone to err as we are to do extraordinary things. We are the result of both humanity's greatest accomplishments and pitfalls. It's normal to analyze and filter all the information we receive in order to relate it to what's around us. It's normal to prefer those dear to us over strangers. It's normal to like and dislike certain qualities in other people.

Most of the time, our judgements are based on what people do or have on the surface. For example, we may know someone who owns a luxury car and a mansion, so we might feel the teeth of envy chewing away at us. Little do we know about the sleepless nights they might be spending away from their families or the stress involved in running a large-scale business in order to reach that level of wealth. If we knew all that went on behind-the-scenes, we might not be so tempted to switch places with the people we envy.

I'd like to propose an exercise: Let's imagine that the person you're about to judge looks you in the eye and says, "You think you know what I've done, but you don't have a clue about what I've been through." Maybe then we'll stop and think for a minute, just enough to recall that once upon a time, we have also found ourselves facing inner struggles so deep that only God knows about them—and that there were moments when we needed compassion, if not understanding.

Perhaps in those situations, something should change within us, at least in circumstances that demanded it. For example, most of us have probably heard negative comments about ones who have passed. When someone leaves this world forever, the bad parts should also be laid to rest, so that only good thoughts remain, channeled towards those left behind – if not for common decency, then at least for the sake of shared humanity.

The Most Beautiful Snowdrops

A few days ago, I saw a little girl selling snowdrops in the street. I'd never seen such beautiful flowers in my entire life! I thought of my girls waiting for me at home, and naturally, I approached the girl to buy some.

A lady who'd just bought a bunch of flowers from her was waiting for the change for the 10 lei (Romanian currency) she'd handed over. The little girl confidently gave her 5 lei back and moved on. The lady bluntly said, "Come on, give me another 2 lei. Be fair!" The little girl smiled timidly and took a roll of banknotes out of her pocket.

When it was my turn, I asked her where she got the snowdrops, and she said she picked them in the forest with her father. I asked for three bunches and handed her a 10 lei banknote and some ones. She smiled as timidly as she had to the lady before and asked, "How much am I supposed to give you back?" At that moment, I realized that the sweet little girl didn't know how to add, so the lady had judged her unfairly.

Pluto and Saturn

It is so important to realize that every person you meet is superior to you in at least one area. This truism has various benefits:

- It helps you maintain decency and common sense.
- It protects you from arrogance.
- It can dramatically mitigate your sense of inferiority about someone who may crush you with their personality or attitude. In turn, we are certainly superior to them in at least one area.

My oldest daughter Ruxandra wrote this story about this concept when she was nine:

"No one noticed Pluto because it was the smallest planet in the solar system. In fact, it is so small that if an asteroid hit it, it would roll over like a bowling ball!

So, Saturn used to tease it, and Pluto replied, 'I may be small, but I have a great soul! You don't judge a person by their size, but by their heart!'

The planets started laughing at her, and Pluto left, embarrassed and upset.

One night, Pluto heard Saturn crying for help. She soon saw what was going on: Saturn was being hit by some small asteroids, and Pluto told them to leave him alone.

'Thank you, Pluto!' Saturn said. 'From here on out, I will not tease you!'

And that's how it was from then on! Saturn told the other planets about the incident, and Pluto became friends with all the planets, including the Sun.

That's why it's better to be friendly than arrogant, and not to laugh at an ugly person because they might have a beautiful soul. One shouldn't judge a book by its cover."

Jesus Himself advised us: "Do not judge for not being judged!"

Chapter 2: Cures

"For every evil, there are two cures: Time and Silence."

Alexander Dumas

Hasn't everyone in this world received a terrible blow at some point in time? One of those hits might be so painful that it leaves you breathless. Someone once said there are two types of pain: one that hurts and another that transforms. I will focus on the latter.

Do you remember the exact moment when you lost someone dear to you? Or a time when you were badly hurt by a loved one? These kinds of moments are usually the ones responsible for transfixing wounds, which result in deep scars that even plastic surgery can't fix. It's only natural; if you have no expectations of someone, they can't hurt you. So, the ones you trust – and whom you have allowed into your heart – have acquired this capability in full! The times when you receive a terrible blow trigger an intense dyspnea of the soul, which bears a close resemblance to the feeling of imminent death experienced by patients having a heart attack.

I can still clearly remember the agonizing moments when I waited outside the operating room, where my wife was in hemorrhagic shock. It was a few hours after she gave birth to our youngest daughter. Under the overwhelming weight of fear, everything seemed to crumble into pieces around me. Its chill haunted me while she was in a coma for five days.

In such circumstances, we feel our soul being crushed by a burden we aren't sure we can carry, and a devastating pain consumes our entire being. Everything falls apart around us as we collapse. We pray to God to spare us from these intense pangs. This metastasis seems to have left nothing good in us. And in His great kindness, He hears us and sends us two therapeutic solutions: Silence and Time.

Silence

Our entire beings are in turmoil during times of adversity and strife. We are like rice in boiling water, and we feel a terrible urge to free ourselves from built-up negative energy. But with all this pressure, our vocal cords are at a standstill, under the anesthetic force of pain; it is so powerful that we are left with aphasia and speechlessness.

Sometimes, we experience silence as a reflexive form of defense, but it often manifests itself as a way to punish those who wronged us, because silence is associated with indifference. And indifference hurts even more than resentment or hatred.

Some lyrics come to mind from "When You Don't Speak" by Romanian poet Adrian Paunescu:

I never know. I never know
What you listen to when you don't speak.
My eyes gaze at you, and they have fallen down
on their knees.

But you keep your silence. But you keep your silence.

There is void and forgetfulness and cold between us,

Only when you are silent...

Many times, our silence speaks volumes...

Time

Time's unrelenting passing fills in gaps created in our souls by those who once took bites out of them. If wounds are deep, it will take time for the soul to regain its peacefulness. Painful memories occasionally create insatiable whirlpools that ransack the peace of heartstrings that dwell in the deep. Then as time passes, their power becomes increasingly shallow, so we become more serene. Many times, this effect happens even faster than we might expect. Romanian poet Nichita Stanescu once wrote, "If time had leaves, what an autumn that would be!"

Sooner or later, peace will settle over it all; sooner or later, it will settle. We'll once again know its warm embrace because all things grow over time, except suffering...

Tired soul

It's certainly true that the soul is weak from time to time. Sometimes, this weakness can seemingly occur out of the blue. Other times, a varying amount of discontentment builds up gradually, and the soul starts feeling burdened under its load. When that happens, people can feel exhausted, even tired of living. Then it's as if nothing makes sense, and we feel attacked by self-deception and her older sister, depression.

In those moments, it's vital to be someone who has cast heavy anchors into the ocean of life: to have a family and a home, and to be a respected in your community and your profession. These constants can bring you whirring back to life and pull you out of the muck of negative energy.

In the end, it's all a matter of mentally whipping yourself into shape (although it's better to be kind to yourself beforehand than to whip yourself afterward). Imagine yourself during one of those depressing moments when you feel depleted of power. Everywhere you look, everything is bleak around you, and your insides become very Bacovian.[1]

All day long, you are overwhelmed by a feeling of fatigue. But then you get home one evening, and you find out you have won the lottery: $10 million! What would your reaction be? Obviously, you will be enveloped by a feeling of fantastic energy—like the wings of a Pegasus have grown out of your back. And just a couple of minutes ago, you had plummeted to the ground—like Icarus after the wax in his wings melted.

No matter how strong the driving energies are that enliven us throughout life, there are sufficient moments when the soul gets tired, and our actions and the actions of those around us lose their oomph and moral firmness. So, I think it's better to occasionally indulge ourselves and people around us. In the end,

---

[1]Bacovia was a Romanian poet who romanticized depression.

we're all just souls in transit, not in competition with each other...

Lemon or lemonade

When life hands you over a lemon, make a lemonade!

Building on the musings of Dale Carnegie, I will add: 'You can find honey in the family and with friends.' With this in mind, I sent a text of the famous line to a group, and the most ingenious answer belonged to Gabriela, a former resident. It read something like this: 'I say, let's take salt from friends. I'll bring the tequila. We'll take the lemon from day-to-day life.' What a delicious reply, isn't it?

It's not easy, I admit, to control the squirm of your face and maintain a smile when you drink lemon juice. We are humans, not robots, so resetting usually takes more time. The better we feel in the midst of our family or among friends, the faster the click on the reset command...and the faster we can smile.

And that's not all. Ideally, the smile would be genuine, that is a 100% expression of the soul because they do say a smile is the mirror to the soul. Out of the 18 types of smiles identified by Paul Ekman, only the Duchene smile is authentic. It's the one that also drives the orbicularis oculi muscle into motion, which is the only one connected to the soul (just my opinion, not supported by clinical studies). Other smiles are just used to stand on ceremony, used in varied circumstances and for social convenience because that's what our brain dictates.

The urge of Dale Carnegie can be outlined in another form: it does not matter what happens to us in life, but how we react to situations we face. Instead of making our mouths sour from the lemon, we can turn it into a delicious drink. And if we can't change absolutely anything of what besieges us, well, we do have a possibility to follow the advice of "anonymous": "I am glad when it rains, because, if I weren't glad, it would still rain."

Carpe Diem

Tomorrow is the most important thing in life. Very clean, it comes to us at midnight. It's perfect when it arrives, and it puts itself in our hands. It hopes we've learned something from yesterday.

I would add to John Wayne's statement that today is like a fragile suspension bridge between yesterday and tomorrow. Therefore, let's not climb on it burdened either by past sufferings or future worries because our present will collapse. In the end, today is actually the tomorrow we worried about yesterday.

You've probably heard the old adage that an ounce of prevention is worth a pound of cure. However, we shouldn't let that concept prevent us from enjoying our lives.

Ideally, the importance of today should be realized as soon as possible. Whether or not we let ourselves become overwhelmed by our burdens from the past or worries about tomorrow, the emotions from both are experienced today – not yesterday or tomorrow. While happy memories and an optimistic viewpoint about the future can be helpful, the present is always more important, since that's when experiences actually happen.

No matter how bad it was, the present defeats the past. Nothing can compare to the power of a live experience, when all the receptors in our bodies are intensely excited! But we also have the capacity to bring fragments of the past to the foreground of our conscience, which can make it seem like it's happening again.

Since we cannot know what tomorrow brings, we must fight for our happiness today. So, let's focus on the good things in our lives right now, instead of saying, "Leave it for tomorrow. I don't have time today!" You know why? Today, we don't have the time. Tomorrow, we won't have the strength. And the day after tomorrow, we could cease to exist.

Therefore, I think it would be best if we could sweep the three hypostases – past, present and future – with our thoughts and feelings, and not get stuck in one single variant to address the passing of time. In the end, stiffness is for rocks, not for humans!

A Fearful Ending

I was performing my rounds in the hospital, and one of the patients was anxious about a colonoscopy, as he'd had rectal bleeding for months. I told him: "A fearful ending is better than endless fear! Why keep a nail in your brain that will become harder and harder to cope with?" Unfortunately, his ending was indeed fearsome: The source of bleeding turned out to be a rectal cancer, but it was easily treatable, since it was caught early.

Intelligent Threshold

With this story in my mind, I think that a nail stuck in the sole is more easily coped with than a nail driven into the brain or the heart!

I've had my fair share of nails in my brain and my soul, just like everyone else. At first sight, the difference between the intensity of an acute pain caused by a lesion and the intensity of a chronic pain endured by our soul or brain contradicts the above musing, especially if the person concerned is intelligent.

Researchers at Wake Forest University theorized that your level of intelligence is inversely proportional to the threshold of our sensitivity to pain. In other words, the smarter you are, the more intense your perception of physical pain will be. So, the next time a toothache drives you crazy, you should be able to alleviate your own pain at the mere thought that you are a very intelligent person.[2]

But things are not that simple at all. In the end, the brain is the one managing pain, especially since its intensity depends on the cortical representation of the

---

[2]Have you seen *Lost in Translation*? In that movie, many jokes are made that no one gets due to the language barrier. In an effort to make sure all readers are in on the jokes in this book, I've added an emoji to accentuate the punchlines. It's reminiscent of two things:

- This book's origins in social media.
- The vaudeville acts of Eastern Europe, which used a classic snare drum and cymbal to ensure laughs from the audience: Bah Dum Dum Crish!

organ where nervous impulses are produced. The elbow, for example, has few nociceptor terminals (those that send painful impulses), and here is where the expression "Ma doare in cot!" (TN: a word for word translation is "it's like an elbow ache for me" meaning "I don't care a fig for it!" or "It's nothing to me!"). Instead, the heart occupies vast cerebral territories, so that a nail driven in it by a friend, lover or someone close to us will produce an intense experience because of reverberations that will significantly amplify the pain. Moreover, since it is provided with a very good memory (after all, it is a feminine gender noun – translated in Romanian it is), the heart will regularly have to cope with the terrible action of the hammer of memories, the one that, once primed, will fiercely drive nails into it, shredding it to pieces.

As if that were not enough, the brain itself suffers from a chronic anxious disorder – and we ourselves will implant nails in our souls without reason and bear painful burdens as a result of various thoughts and dramatic scenarios we imagine we might be forced to face. Even Mark Twain encountered a pile of mishaps throughout his life, some of which actually happened.

Therefore, the lesson here is to not envy people who seem to be physically intact because we might never know how many nails they have had driven through their heart during their life and how many tears they have wept and will weep.

Feather, leaf and desert

As a physician, I benefit from the privilege of being aware of the frailty inside our bodies to a greater extent than other professions. Young people, in whom the flame of life was burning brightly, got in their car one morning to warm up another day in their journey on this earth and that of their dear ones. Some hours later, their family's entire castle of dreams was shattered among contorted irons under the lethal crush of a car driven by a show-off.

By the way, do you know what is the most dangerous car? In my opinion, there is nothing comparable to a car driven by a young man who has a girl in his right seat and who wants to impress her. (I have already drawn my daughter's attention to this perspective, so that she will know how to react if she happens to find herself in such a situation.)

Therefore, it is essential to become aware of what wise men of old days said, not only once: we are like leaves! Beyond the serenity acceptance of our destiny, at one point, each of us gets their turn to leave this earth. It happens that the end of a leaf won't coincide with its withering. There are those cases when a leaf crushes together with the tree in which the scythe of destiny has driven its sharp edge, and the tally can be read only beyond the skies. There are those circumstances when a strong individual beside us – be it a husband, a wife, a parent or a child – is taken from us suddenly, as I have witnessed so many times in the hospital.

While I was creating the picture of this leaf called man, I had a flashback with the start of one of the best films of all times: *Forest Gump*. It's that white feather the wind plucks out from near the hero's feet and blows it, tossing it here and there, without a definite destination. Referring to *Forest Gump*, the protagonist's mother said, "Life is like a box of chocolates. You never know what you're going to get." Therefore, one should not wait for a perfect moment to have dessert. When there's an imperfect moment passing us by, we should seize it, make it perfect, and indulge!

God's Brick

"A young man was driving his new Jaguar in a region that didn't have a good reputation, so he was driving faster than usual. However, he was paying attention to the road, so he could avoid obstacles such as careless children. At one point, he saw something moving, so he slowed down. Out of nowhere, a brick struck the door of his Jaguar.

Extremely angry, he pulled over, jumped out of his car, and discovered a little boy nearby. He scooped the boy up, pushed him up against the back of a nearby car, and screamed:

'What did you do that for? Who do you think you are? This is a new car, and the brick you threw has caused serious damage. Why did you do that?'

To defend himself, the boy said: 'Please, sir, please! I ask for forgiveness, but I didn't know what else to do. I threw the brick because no one else would stop.' With tears flowing down his cheeks, the boy pointed to a spot behind a parked car. 'There is my brother. Someone hit him. His wheelchair tipped over on the sidewalk, and he fell out of it. But I cannot lift him by myself.'

The boy asked the young man, 'Can you please help me put my brother back in his chair?'

The driver was dumbfounded. He quickly placed the crippled boy back in his wheelchair and helped clean the boy's wounds. With one glance, he realized that his injuries were only surface wounds, so they would heal quickly.

'Thank you! God bless you!' the first boy said gratefully.

The driver stood on the sidewalk and watched the boy push his brother away in the wheelchair.

Then he returned to his Jaguar. The damage was pretty major, but the young man never had the car repaired. He left it that way to remind himself of the following message: 'Don't live your life so fast that you force others to throw a brick and draw your attention!'

God whispers in our souls and speaks to our hearts. Sometimes, when we don't have time to listen to Him, he throws a brick at us. Then it's our choice whether we listen to Him or not..."

Chapter 3: Generosity

"I do not know any other sign of superiority but kindness."
Beethoven

In fact, generosity is the easiest way to diagnose love, which is the quintessence of humanity. The Apostle Paul concurred in his First Epistle to the Corinthians: "And now these three remain: faith, hope, and love. But the greatest of these is love."

"Ask not what your country can do for you. Ask what you can do for your country!" When JFK made this statement during his inaugural address, it electrified many people. This reversal of the direction of action—from the inside to the outside, in terms of intrinsic forces that lead our being—could move mountains! It is so important to build bridges between ourselves and others! We can use them to send messages from our souls and spirits.

The foundations of these bridges would be so much more solid if we developed the habit of regularly asking those around us: "How can I help you?" – a question that might ignite a light in others' eyes. But many times, the centripetal force that governs our thoughts, feelings, and actions is stronger than the centrifugal force directed towards others, which is actuated by empathy and generosity.

Consequently, the light in their eyes will gradually turn off, and we can even hear them humming Dan Spataru's love song: "I won't knock on closed doors anymore. Don't be ashamed, and don't turn your eyes away from me." As we tend to act due to centripetal forces rather than centrifugal ones, we are not able to offer help to our friends anymore. Therefore, the light within their eyes will gradually fade, and they won't come back to us to ask for help again, since they assume that the gates to our souls are closed.

My Utmost for His Highest

A man is never greater than when he bends down to help someone whom life has thrown to the ground. Yes, perhaps we get shorter during those moments, but our soul rises up to meet God in all His splendor. It doesn't matter whether others see us or not; what's important is that He sees us. Then we will find Heaven Within, as our inner selves will know the contentment that naturally emerges when we support our fellow men.

I have reached this conclusion for some time now: People willing to offer others pieces of their time (and ultimately, their lives) without expecting something in return are not common. But when you see them, you can easily recognize them by the scrapes on their knees – from the innumerable occasions when they have knelt down to help those who've fallen down. These are the people who care! You should keep these special people close by, as they will bless our lives with their mere presence.

They say a winner doesn't feel pain when he's wounded. But true winners are recruited from the ranks of those who care about others, because these

32

people feel even the pain of the competition they've defeated.

Mirror Neurons

Researchers have recently identified a special class of neurons in the brain. These "mirror neurons" play essential roles in guessing the emotions of individuals we interact with, especially their capacity for empathy. To varying degrees, these neurons are responsible for manifesting kindness.

I could swear that Ruxandra's brain is only made of mirror neurons! I have rarely seen a more generous child. Since she was barely a year old, she has amazed us with her generosity. She would not keep anything in her own hands if another child asked her for it. Even Mu, a stuffed cow she has slept with since she was six months old, would turn up in the arms of one of her friends if they asked her for it.

The Good Seminarian

In his book *Social Intelligence*, Daniel Goleman presents an extremely interesting study conducted at a theological school in England. The study documented 40 students who weren't aware they were part of the study. They were expecting to deliver a short sermon to be graded. Half of them were told to preach about the Good Samaritan, and the other half were assigned to preach about a variety of topics.

The seminarians all gathered in an amphitheater, and one of them would leave to give his sermon in another building every fifteen minutes.

Along the way, they had to pass a room where a man was lying on the ground and groaning in pain. Out of the 40 students, 24 of them completely ignored the groaning man.

It turned out that the seminarians who had been assigned to preach about the Good Samaritan were more willing than the other students to stop and help the man.

Time was also extremely important to the seminarians. Out of the ten who thought they would be late for their sermon, only one of them stopped. But of the ten seminarians who thought they had plenty of time, six stopped and offered to help.

This study shows that most people feed their ego, which continually fills their ears with the idea that others should gravitate around them. We are endowed with the instinct of survival, which insists on soliciting us to solve our own issues first, then direct our attention to those around us.

Furthermore, ego can easily be compared to a stomach. If it's empty, our capacity to focus on other actions is seriously disrupted by abdominal noises, which alert us that we should feed ourselves! Consecutively, the centrifugal force that externalizes the thoughts, feelings, and attitudes that are positively reflected in others becomes pretty anemic, so our focus on them is usually too frail, in terms of time.

The Validation Network

We all long for three magical words that start with "A": appreciation, acceptance, approval. I think this reality is fundamental to the unimaginable success that Facebook has achieved. I call it a "validation network," rather than a social network. We all know what devastating effects it's had on true human interaction, but these three A's have a hungry craving for acknowledgement that is evidenced in our desire for more likes.

Pay It Forward

Probably the only person who hates the idea that he shall sow what he reaps is a boxer, who prefers this motto: "It's better to give than to receive!"

While most people get this joke, those who prefer more elegant language might prefer this way of expressing the same sentiment: a bit of fragrance always lingers in the hand that gives the flower.

At one point, Romanian monk Arsenie Boca made this deep remark: *In the beginning, we give what we have, but eventually, we'll give what we are.* We don't even have to give very much, as long as our gesture comes from the heart. It's better to give little things with love than to do great things out of self-interest. In order to have beautiful eyes, one does not need to pluck their eyebrows, powder their faces, or wear contact lenses. It's enough to see the good in others. And in order to have beautiful lips, one does not need to wear lipstick or resort to plastic surgery. It's enough to utter beautiful words.

This train of thought reminds me of the great movie *Pay It Forward*. The protagonist is a 10-year-old kid who comes up with the idea that each individual should help three people in need, without getting anything in return. The only condition to those being helped is that they, in turn, need to help three other people in distress, without receiving anything in return for their gesture. Ultimately, kindness would increase exponentially!

An Originator of Generosity

Undoubtedly, the boy in *Pay It Forward* was original. It reminds of the phrase: *Always strive to be the first: the first to forgive, the first to accept, the first to smile, the first to say a soothing word, the first who gives.*

Sometimes, generosity can seem paradoxical to success: If you want to be in first place, you can't be the first one to give, because it will be a sign of weakness. However, someone who wishes to outperform and win at all costs is much less likely to experience inner peace. It's hard to accept something that doesn't sit well with you if your soul isn't at peace. The fierceness of those who always want to be in first place inescapably alters the generosity they were born with. The fight to reach the top often results in casualties: those who are left behind, abandoned or walked all over – and common sense cannot accept this kind of an attitude. After all, there is room under the sun for everyone, especially since most of us want to stay in the shade!

Look at the today's great leaders of the world: are all of them monuments of genuine kindness and generosity? Can you imagine them ever extending a sign of remorse or an admission of wrongdoing? I sincerely doubt it!

But now think about the great spiritual leaders of the world, such as Jesus, Mother Theresa, and Pope John Paul II. The mere image of them is sufficient to envelop our souls in the quietness we all need to face the chaos of life. Because all the gentle ones are good...

True perfume

The true perfume is on the hand of man who offers the flower.

One of the longest roads many of us travel in life is the one between ME and THE OTHERS. This is because from childhood we acquire the maxim "All roads lead to Rome" as if each and everyone of us would be called Rome. And our expectations will be to the measure: everything must be sucked to us with the force of a tornado, like those we see in the United States! Who could stand against such a calamity? I don't use this word by accident – frustrations that we assimilate through the years seeing that there are also other cities besides Rome can devastate us at an emotional level many a times...

Life is God's gift to the human race, and the way we live it is our gift to those around us. The gifts may look like presents under a Christmas tree that generates excitement and are joyfully opened. But sadly, we could also offer empty boxes, since we prefer to fill our boxes instead of others' boxes. Let's not get into these kinds of situations! In interpersonal relationships, we're all millionaires. But what we do with this wealth is up to us. We can share it, or hoard it for ourselves like misers. In the end, it's not what we've collected, but what we've shared that truly matters. And there's no way there isn't some perfume left on the hand of the one who gave a bunch of flowers...

Cherished Antiques

She gave me her pennies

Hidden in a handkerchief,
And she stood at the gate
Looking back sad.
In her mind, she wondered,
Will I ever get to see my granddaughter next
year?
On my way home, I could hardly carry
Jam jars and all that she gave me.
Looking through the luggage, I was
confounded
'Cause the heaviest of all was, in fact, love!"

I found this jewel on Facebook, and the picture in the post was of a grandmother standing at a gate. She was that genuine type of grandmother you can find in rural places.

Meanwhile, my Grandmother Maria lived only for her children, grandchildren, and great-grandchildren. For over 20 years, the many members of this side of my family filled the void that remained after she lost my grandfather and Uncle John, her youngest son, who died from a terrible disease at 52.

About a year ago, Ruxandra and I paid her a visit. When we left, she saw us off. But I'd only driven for about 2-3 meters when I stopped and backed up.

In the rearview mirror, I'd seen so much love in my grandmother's eyes that I told myself that such an image deserves to be recorded. So I stood by her for another minute and filmed her waving goodbye. She was the epitome of common sense, love and longing!

We would be better off if we treated our elders like they're as cherished as priceless antiques. As the sand falls in the hourglass of life, you can see through it more clearly. They finally know all the answers, but no one asks them for advice any more, even though their knees are buckling under the weight of their experience.

So doesn't it sound like a good idea to start asking the elderly questions? We will certainly find that many of them are open-minded and understanding, since getting old means transitioning from passion to compassion...

The Last Loaf

"During some wars, life was tough and people were hungry. But a rich man decided to help the poor, so he announced he'd give free bread to all the children from village. The next day, many people gathered in the courtyard on the side of the man's house. When he appeared with large baskets full of bread, the children rushed over, shoving and hitting each other, so they could grab as much bread as possible. It was an unspeakable act.

But the man noticed a little girl waiting at the edge of the courtyard. After all the other children had chosen what they wanted and gone, the little girl approached a basket and looked into it, but there was nothing left. Then she looked in the second basket, but it was also empty. She was overjoyed she when found a small piece of bread at the bottom of the third basket; no one else had noticed it. The little girl thanked the man for the bread and went home.

For the rest of the day, the man thought about the girl's behavior. That night, he ordered the cook to bake more bread, but to put 10 coins in one of the smaller loaves. Then in the morning, he placed the loaf at the bottom of one of the basket, and took all of the baskets into the courtyard, where the children had already gathered. Again, they rushed to the baskets and fought each other to get bigger pieces of bread.

In the end, our little girl (who had again been quietly waiting) took the only remaining loaf – the smallest one. Once again, she thanked the man and hurried home, where her mother was waiting for her. When they sat down at the table, she broke the bread, and the coins fell onto the table.

'Wow, look at all this money, 'the woman said, a little fearfully. 'What if the baker accidentally dropped that man's money in here while she was kneading the dough, and he comes looking for it? Take the coins and return them to him!'

The little girl returned to the rich man's house, gave him all the money back, and told him that her mother had found them in her bread. Looking at her lovingly, the man replied:

'That money did not happen to just make it into your bread on accident. After seeing how you had patience to wait and how content you were with less, I decided to reward you. Today, I've seen how honest you are. You could have kept the money, but you brought it back. As a reward, every morning when you come to get some bread, you'll also get ten gold coins!'

The girl was overjoyed. She didn't know how to thank this man for such kindness. She ran home, gave her mother the money, and told her everything. But her mother instructed her about what to do, and the girl followed her advice.

So every morning when she received the coins, she shared them with the other children, since she knew others needed charity as much as she did..."

Chapter 4: Optimism

"Results may be the same, be it you are an optimist or a pessimist, but optimists feel better..."
Anonymous

It wasn't a coincidence that the only thing left in Pandora's Box was hope. But for pessimists, hope evaporates like a drop of water in the Sahara! The lack thereof weighs so heavily on the soul that even the corners of their mouth are pointing downwards.

By design, human beings are social entities. Daily interactions leave their marks on individuals via fairly subtle mechanisms. Some pessimists might feel good in their "I told you so!" shoes, but most of the time, their attitude touches those around them and impacts their moods. And since the nocebo effect (anticipating negative side effects) is stronger than the placebo effect (anticipating positive benefits), we are more easily contaminated by an incurable pessimist than by someone in a good mood.

I, for one, would rather talk to an optimist who's been wrong a hundred times than a pessimist who's right all the time. This statement is not an invitation to ignorance, of course. Each of us has his or her own value system and life experience that allows us to assess a situation. But in my case, I must admit that my life operates better when it's bathed in a positive tone.

Beyond its negative effects on some organs, I believe alcohol acts on specific cell groups, such as the ones that produce sadness, quietness and memory. But the impact on them is selective: Sadness cells are damaged in optimists (who get to see their lives through rose-colored glasses), whereas quietness cells are damaged in realists (who start wagging their tongues). While pessimists try to drown their bitterness in alcohol, the memory cells that are stimulated keep all the black memories they're trying to escape from alive.

Should our optimism collapse at a certain point, we should also take a realistic look at the situation we find ourselves in before surrendering to the hands of pessimism. Why? Very simple: For a realist, it really doesn't matter if the glass is half-empty or half-full. Rather, what matters is what's left in the bottle, and if the bottle can be refilled!

A Smile Is the Kiss of the Soul

I'm going to ask you to analyze the people around you whom you most frequently encounter. I would like you to break them down into two groups: those who smile a lot, and those who smile very little. Write their names on separate pieces of paper, and try to visualize them one at a time. Pay attention to the mood these individuals induce in you. It's amazing when we realize what a rapid impact recalled faces have, let alone your direct interaction with them!

But why do we lose so many smiles as we age? Look at how much more frequently children smile than adults! On average, a child smiles 250 times a day. A woman, 56 times. And a man, only 8 times. If we were to compare smiles to most characteristic traits, we could easily conclude that kids are optimistic, and adults are pessimistic. An old Chinese proverb says that we are born wet, naked and hungry; after that, things get worse!

Why is that? Is it because we lose our innocence? Or is it because everything that's revealed to us throughout the years is no longer as sweet as it was in childhood? Is it that every blow we get in life slowly erases our smile? Or do they gradually eat away at our soul? Because that's what a smile is: a kiss of the soul. In contrast, a smile moves other souls with a delicate touch that only someone light and unburdened can offer.

Out of the 18 types of smiles that are out there, only one is genuine. A soul that has received major blows throughout the years may have lost some of its teeth. But if your soul knew how to keep or regenerate its impeccable dentures, your smile can still be charming, even if you have no teeth left in your mouth!

Among other things, a smile is an expression of a subconscious message that the person displaying it doesn't pose a threat – that any aggressiveness is completely superficial. That's probably one reason why women smile seven times more than men.

Have You Made Someone Smile Today?

This is the title of <u>one of the most beautiful videos</u> ever posted online.[3] Basically, it's the story of Hugh, a mall employee who validates parking tickets, but also who compliments every single driver by pointing out something positive, no matter how small, in each one. At one point, one of the security agents from the building went to his boss, alarmed, and said, "Come quickly. We have a problem!"

Instead of parking and walking to the mall, people were standing in a queue to validate their parking tickets. They were actually trying to get Hugh to emotionally validate them. They would leave the booth with their faces bathed in smiles.

The video is extraordinary. It's really worth spending – no, *investing* – 15 minutes of your time. Right now!

Smile While You Can

We are born crying, and we die surrounded by mourning. The only option left is to live smiling, because a smile makes the heart happy. The

[3] <u>https://www.youtube.com/watch?v=aTBXfwKTBkI</u>

45

extraordinary thing about a smile is that it can make its recipient wealthy without impoverishing the person who gave it. Many times, it only lasts for a second, but its memory remains instilled in our mind for a long time.

Nobody is so rich that they can afford to ignore a smile, and nobody is so poor that they cannot give it to others. Mind you, life's moments pass like the speed of light. So smile while you still have teeth left!

The 1%

After 20 years, a mountaineer managed to conquer Everest. Coming down from there, more dead than alive, someone asked him, "Why did you go there? To die?" The climber replied: "No, I went there to live!"

There are two categories of people: realists and dreamers. Realists know where they are heading; dreamers are already there because they never get tired of their dreams! We need people, who are animated by that passion which sets in motion the creative energies that have given and will continue to give rise to the progress of humanity, whether we refer to spiritual, moral or technical. Of ten people who speak, there is one who thinks; of ten people who think, there is one who acts. Of those1% are the passionate people. They are not satisfied with a passing existence (I participate, but I do not go!) These are the people who have a dream that they

46

follow with ardor, so much so that he does not find the woman of dreams in the meantime – because then, they'd have to say goodbye to their other dreams!

I'm just poking fun at examples we've had over history, of men whose spirit was decisively animated by the love for the women in their lives: For 20 years, Ulysses needed to return to Penelope, ending her pain of trusting and waiting for him. The work of Mihai Eminescu was mainly born out of the fire that burnt in his heart for Veronica Micle.[4] And let's not forget about Dante Alighieri and Beatrice. The latter had Alighieri mesmerized from adolescence. For her, he "exited the fog of the many" and obeyed his solemn pledge to write things about her that had never been written before.

There are passions that enter our lives like red-hot flames, and they are never extinguished. They will sizzle, day in and day out, hemmed in the scorching heat conveyed by undertaking them. It can be the infatuation that begins when a young lover meets his soulmate, a scientist's spirit itching for knowledge, or the unquenchable desire to overcome our limits. Whatever the motivation, it is so strong that all the cells of the body will resonate in unison in the fulfillment of our destinies.

---

[4]Mihai Eminescu was a Romanian poet, novelist, and journalist, generally regarded as the most influential Romanian writer of all time.

If we really want something, we will find a way; if not, we will find an excuse, says popular wisdom. If at the end, we realize that it was not possible to reach the destination we wanted so badly, what really matters is that along the way to fulfilling our dreams, we have known the passion that makes us feel that we are living – not just merely existing. Men age when worries replace dreams, and my dream is to die young at an old age.

A Diamond in the Rough

For months, Michelangelo searched high and low until he found the marble for sculpting his statue of David. The moment the statue was unveiled, strong emotions overwhelmed the crowd of people which had gathered in the plaza in Florence. After being asked how he managed to sculpt such a marvel, the master answered: "It wasn't that hard. I looked within David, and all I had to do was remove all that was not him."

In every moment of our existence, let us be aware that a better alternative lies deep down inside us, and it's only up to us to bring it to light. Yes, each of us is a rough stone that must be ground, polished and buffed. Handled forcefully and wisely – with God's guidance – the chisel and hammer will finally manage to bring the beauty and brightness of our inner diamond to the surface! Because we are not what we are. We are what we can be!

Chapter 5: Spirituality

"Here I am! I stand at the door and knock. If anyone hears My voice and opens the door, I will come in and eat with that person, and they with Me."
Revelation 3:20

Imitatio Christi by Thomas de Kempis is a wonderful book that enlightened my student years. Aside from the extraordinary content of this book, I remember the outstanding impact that its cover had on me! It's a picture of Christ standing before a door, ready to knock. I don't think any other painting (not even the renowned "Light of the World" by William Holman Hunt) has captured the humbleness, delicacy and gentleness of the Messiah as He comes to offer humankind a supreme gift, the Kingdom of God.

Did you let Him in?

While I haven't been able to find the painting from that book cover anywhere online, Hunt's painting is prominently displayed in a museum. At one point, a group of tourists expressed their admiration for this splendid work of art. One admired the color scheme; another noticed the expression on the Messiah's face, and others observed that the door had no handle on the outside. Only a child asked the essential question: "Daddy, in the end, did they let Him in?"

It wasn't an accident that Christ used to say, "Let the children come to me!" This is what God wants for us: to bear light souls, not souls burdened with the heavy weight of sin. Only then can our souls raise up to His Kingdom, and unite with Christ; this is the only way to redeem ourselves.

When God banished Adam and Eve from the Garden of Eden, the course of humankind changed dramatically. The meaning of this moment has been passed on from generation to generation, by both wise men and ordinary people, in both books and in everyday conversations. The idea of original sin created by Adam's decision-making in the Garden has caused some people to feel like they need to continuously have a penitent relationship with God. But one of the main reasons for Christ's return was to change this mindset; it can be very counterproductive, especially in countries like Romania, which have experienced a tremendous amount of economic adversity.

Some Eastern Europeans have taken this separation anxiety to an extreme, such as Anton Chekhov, who asserts in his play *Uncle Vanya* that life is nothing more than a continuous penance until we are reunited with God in heaven: "We will hear the angels, we will see the whole sky, all diamonds, we will see how all earthly evil, all our sufferings, are drowned in the mercy that will fill the whole world. And our life will grow peaceful, tender, sweet as a caress. You have had no joy in your life; but wait, Uncle Vanya, wait! We will rest..."

I believe that there is no reason to wait for the afterlife to feel heaven in our lives. Yes, God drove

Adam and Eve out of the Garden of Eden, but He also sent His Son to die for our sins. In support of this Good News, I would like to remind you of Jesus' statement in Luke 17: 21: "Why wait to be with Him in the afterlife when you can find Heaven Within You right now?"

Wait!

God works in mysterious ways, and our mind is much too obtuse to be able to penetrate His wisdom. One of the most beautiful dialogues between a Christian, who is tired of having so many unanswered questions, and a God, who "justifies" His attitude, can be found in the poem "Wait" by an anonymous Romanian author:

> *Desperately, helplessly, longingly, I cried:*
> *Quietly, patiently, lovingly God replied.*
> *I pled and I wept for a clue to my fate,*
> *And the Master so gently said, "Child, you*
> *must wait."*
>
> *"Wait? You say, wait!" my indignant reply.*
> *"Lord, I need answers, I need to know why!*
> *Is your hand shortened? Or have you not*
> heard?*
> *By faith, I have asked, and am claiming your*
> *Word.*
>
> *My future and all to which I can relate*
> *Hangs in the balance, and YOU tell me to*
> WAIT?*
> *I'm needing a "yes," go ahead and sign,*

51

Or even a "no" to which I can resign.
And Lord, You promised that if we believe
We need but to ask, and we shall receive.
And Lord, I've been asking, and this is my cry:
"I'm weary of asking! I need a reply!"

Then quietly, softly, I learned of my fate
As my Master replied once again, "You must wait."
So I slumped in my chair, defeated and taut.
And grumbling to God, "So, I'm waiting... for what?"
He seemed, then, to kneel, and His eyes wept with mine,

And He tenderly said, "I could give you a sign.
I could shake the heavens, and darken the sun.
I could raise the dead, and cause mountains to run.
All you seek, I could give, and pleased you would be.
You would have what you want, but you wouldn't know Me.

You'd not know the depth of My love for each saint;
You'd not know the power that I give to the faint;
You'd not learn to see through the clouds of despair;
You'd not learn to trust just by knowing I'm there;

You'd not know the joy of resting in Me
When darkness and silence were all you could
see.
You'd never experience that fullness of love
As the peace of My Spirit descends like a dove;

You'd know that I give and I save (for a start),
But you'd not know the depth of the beat of My
heart.
The glow of My comfort late into the night,
The faith that I give when you walk without
sight,

The depth that's beyond getting just what you
asked
Of the infinite God, who makes what you have
last
You'd never know, should your pain quickly
flee,
What it means that 'My grace is sufficient for
Thee.'

Yes, your dreams for your loved one overnight
would come true,
But oh the loss if I lost what I'm doing in you!
So be silent, My Child, and in time, you will
see
That the greatest of gifts is to get to know Me.

And though oft' My answers seem terribly late,
My most precious answer is still, 'WAIT.'"

Let us receive God in our souls, and be full of hope and trust. Let us not doubt His infinite love. Let us not despair under the weight of life's burdens. Let us not make Him responsible when some distress comes upon us: "God, God, what have I done wrong for you to punish me so?" God deals the cards, but we play the hands. And if we have the impression that God is silent when we face hardship, let us remember that the best teachers all keep quiet during a test...

Even if things can change in the blink of an eye, God does not blink! Therefore, let us not worry about tomorrow, as God is already there...

The Mentor of My Dreams

One of the most extraordinary people I've ever met was Dr. Radu Ciuchendea, the Head of Medical Clinic I in Sibiu. He was my mentor for six years, and I have rarely seen a more balanced, calmer or more generous person!

Fortunately, I had the chance to be around him during my professional training and personal adjustment to hospital life. Given his substantial emotional intelligence, his interactions with people created an outstanding amount of harmony. In fact, I've never seen him reprimand anyone in public. If he had to reproach someone, he would call them into his office, where he would make calm observations.

Tragically, a serious disease took him away too soon, but maybe it wasn't an accident that I was with him when he breathed his last breath, since we had such a strong connection.

Later, I was the doctor on duty one Sunday afternoon, and the ER was quiet enough for me to take a nap in an exam room. Suddenly, the door swung opened, and Dr. Ciuchendea was standing in the doorway! At the sight of him, I was so surprised that I was struck dumb. My first thought was that he hadn't actually died five months earlier, but had gone to a nursing home for treatment.

Dr. Ciuchendea came close to me and handed me a note that said: "Call Dr. Alexe because she's having a problem with her reflex hammer." He then started examining a patient in another bed of the room. He looked so vibrant in his white lab coat! When he was done with his exam, he came over to me and leaned over, and I hugged him and started crying. At that moment, he disappeared, along with the note.

I started desperately searching for that piece of paper, because I knew no one would believe me when I told them he was actually alive. I needed some evidence!

Then as suddenly as the dream began, I woke up.

Tuesday morning, I bumped into Dr. Alexe when I entered the doctors' lounge. She had just returned from Bucharest, where she took her specialization exam as a gastroenterologist. I started telling her about my dream, and the moment I told her what was written on the note, I saw her change colors.

"Dear me," she said. "You know; I went to Bucharest without my reflex hammer. And on Sunday, when you had the dream, my brother was looking high and low in chemist's shops to buy me one."

Every time I tell story about the dream and get to the part about Dr. Alexe's shocked face, I feel a chill run down my spine!

Fateful Message

One of my former students lost her father to a serious disease while I was teaching her. In an extremely excited state, she posted on Facebook about what happened to her on her father's birthday. She wanted to be alone with her thoughts, so she went for a walk on the streets in Sibiu. Suddenly, she saw a car with a license plate that said, "DADDY LOVES YOU!"

In her post, she said she didn't believe it could be a coincidence. So I invited her to come to the hospital, where I told her about my extraordinary dream about Dr. Ciuchendea.

Some connections are so strong that even passing over to the other side can't break them! I strongly believe that our life does not end when we die. Yes, we return to the dust we came from. However, our journey does not end in the cold, dark earth, but in a bright, warm, green place.

„One evening, tired and discouraged as a result of stressful events, a good Christian sat on his knees, expressing his puzzlement: "Dear God, I am a man afraid of You and I try to follow Your commandments and Your way. Why do You let me swim in troubled waters?" In His infinite wisdom, God replied, "Because your enemies do not know how to swim..."

Part II:

Improving Yourself

Chapter 6: Priorities

"If you don't know where you're headed, any road will take you there."
Anonymous

One of the main reasons for failure in life is wasting time on trifles. Here's the reason why so many people can't manage to do anything in life: When opportunity knocks on their door, they're in the backyard, looking for four-leaf clovers. A common cause for this misguidance is a lack of clear goals. Of course, the people looking for four-leaf clovers will contradict me, saying they do have a clear goal: to find luck. But remember, heaven helps those who help themselves.

Therefore, a list of goals is the first step to creating an ideal future. You can rarely achieve your goals by taking an elevator; most of the time, you have to take the stairs. And since there are a lot of stairs, there's a lot of toil involved in climbing them.

We need to constantly advance ourselves. That's how we stay motivated and get oriented in time and space, with high chances of validating our opportunities. Of course, the road to your castle will be paved with obstacles. In fact, if you don't encounter anything standing in your way, you're probably headed somewhere you shouldn't be going. Therefore, you shouldn't give up if you fail at first.

Strong people stumble many times, but they get up back on their feet. Meanwhile, other people are still crawling around looking for that four-leaf clover.

An Important Responsibility

In addition to being an MD, I'm also an assistent professor. I strongly believe that teachers must convey more to their students than just knowledge about a specific field by providing academic lessons. We must also teach life lessons – why not safeguard them from the trauma we've already experienced?

It's not at all easy to imprint our personal experiences on our students. A child's character isn't like dough; you can't knead it and shape it however you want to. First of all, students come to us with emotional and spiritual baggage from their upbringings, which makes it more difficult to superimpose our values onto the ones they have already assimilated. Secondly, our performances must be convincing enough that they feel safe drinking from our wells of experience. Therefore, a teacher's drive is extremely important in both factors of this equation.

Greetings, Mr. Minister

No matter how gifted you are as a teacher, certain shortcomings can eat away at the channels of communications you have with students. For example, because sometimes teachers in Romania don't have enough money to buy food, the peace required to prepare lessons is often interrupted by growling stomachs.

One of the most colorful jokes that illustrates this idea occurred soon after the management of the Education Ministry was entrusted to a new minister. One day, he entered a grocery store, and an employee immediately approached him and said, "Greetings, Mr. Minister! How are you?'

"How did you recognize me?" the minister asked.

"Well, you know, I used to teach Romanian in secondary school. But the pay is so little, and the psychological strain is so high. So I changed jobs. It's more relaxing, and I earn a better salary here."

After he finished shopping, the minister got into a taxi. The driver already suspected his destination: "The Ministry of Education, right?"

"How did you recognize me?"

"Well, you know, I used to be a university professor. But I was making so little that I changed jobs, and now I make more as a cab driver."

When the minister reached his destination, he saw a beggar at the gate. He approached him to give him some money, and the beggar said: "Greetings, Mr. Minister!

"Don't tell me you used to be a teacher, too?"

"Oh no! I'm currently a teacher, but I have a free period right now."

While this story isn't true, there is a sad reality in Romania that extends beyond nationwide economic difficulties: The government flagrantly disregards the importance of teaching as a profession.

Now consider this: In Japan, teachers are the only citizens who are exempt from bowing before the emperor.

Misguided Baggage

"Long ago, two monks reached the banks of a river, where they saw a woman who wanted to get to the other side. The river could be crossed on foot, but due to strong currents, she was afraid to get into the water. One of the monks offered to help her cross the river by carrying her in his arms, and the woman accepted. When they got on the other side, she thanked him and left.

The two monks continued their journey, and after an hour of smoldering silence, the second monk could no longer refrain from saying, 'I cannot believe what you have done! You carried her in your arms when you know very well that our vows forbid us from touching a woman!'
The first monk sagely replied, 'I set her down an hour ago, but you have carried her with you until now!' "

Meat/Flower/Beast/Angel

A dog saw a girl –

"Meat!" he said, clenching his jaws.
And the girl's parents looked at her –
"Flower!" the parents said, weeping.
And a monk saw her –
"Beast!" the ascetic cried out.
And a poet saw the girl –
"Angel," the poet whispered.

A lot of wisdom can be gathered from this Sanskrit poetry! So many times, we rush to put labels on situations, attitudes and gestures we don't quite understand. While it's human nature to label others, we also label because we rush around like we're running away from Hurricane Katrina!

Even if our label is the fruit of deep analysis, it may still sound like a life sentence without the possibility of parole. We – the self-proclaimed ex cathedra – don't even allow the accused the time to reply. The accused attempts to present his defense from another angle, to no avail. Our value system has spoken. Would anyone dare argue against us? We feel it is a frontal assault. Our wounded pride churns out sentiments and clouds our reasoning, and we become blind to the opposition's truth.

Meanwhile, if we tried looking at our argument through the eyes of the accused, perhaps we would approach the situation differently. For example:

- A pessimist sees the darkness in a tunnel.
- An optimist sees the light at the end of a tunnel.
- A realist sees the lights on the train engine.
- The mechanic sees three lunatics walking on the railroad tracks.

Decisions, Decisions

A disciple asked his teacher, "What do I have to do to get where I want to be?" The master answered, "You must make good decisions, good decisions, good decisions." "How do I do that?"

"Experience, experience, experience." "And how do I gain experience?" "Bad decisions, bad decisions, bad decisions."

See how easy it is to step on the road of life? No matter what path we choose to take when we're at a crossroads, it will still lead us where we should be in the end. Of course, there is one crucial condition for that: to put our faith in God!

The Heart and the Reasoning

The Heart Has Its Own Reasoning, Which Reasoning Does Not Know. Wait a minute! Does this quote by Blaise Pascal mean that one of the most brilliant minds in the history of mankind is acknowledging the superiority of passion over logic? Seems so! Of course, there are differing opinions about this sentiment. Some say that there are no emotions or feelings in the absence of thoughts. Like any reaction in the domain of emotions, its origins invariably occur at the cortical level.

While I don't want to start any arguments, I totally agree with Pascal. For some time, it's been proven that the heart generates an energy field that's 500 times more intense than the brain!

Personally, I always prefer the warm world of feeling to the cold world of thinking. And so does my daughter, Ruxandra: When she was only 5 years old, I asked her: "Love, which one do you reckon is more important: not having a heart or not having a brain?" After a second of pondering, her answer appeared: "Not to have a heart." "Why?" I asked. "Because then you're a bad person."

However, you can put your soul into anything, not just love. It is the soul's mask, also known as passion, which enlivens the entire, complex mechanism that human beings are made of. Passion is the generator of force and tenacity in its attempt to reach its purpose. Thought plots the way to success, but passion is the one things that helps an individual walk the imaginary path that will take you there. So find a way, be passionate about everything you do to make your dreams come true!

I also really like these words by Napoleon Hill: "Success goes through the hearts of people around you. I haven't found another way." So if you want to convince someone to do something, my advice is to touch the hearts of the individuals you want to reach. *People will open their minds to you if you alter their heartbeats...*

Awakening to Life

I will never forget the moment when my wife woke from her coma, after five dark days during which her skin had lost her pallor after undergoing a sever hemorrhage. I was headed toward her room, where she lay intubated, when I saw the smiling face of the nurse caring for my wife. My heart started beating erratically and I rushed inside; the entire room was awash with Gina's tired smile. I started crying uncontrollably, and the accumulated stress of the past few days flowed like a stream from my eyes. My soul – ravaged by terrible thoughts – was instantly reborn.

On the occasion of her baptism, Georgia evoked these moments in a poetic manner:

I stayed in Neonatal for a long time,
With my tiny soul pressed tight,
Because mommy couldn't come
To hold me in my arms, with all her might –
  She was hooked up to a machine.

She was in a coma for days
Statue with inspiration, ready to expire,
Suspended among the stars,
But there still burned a steady fire
  Of the thread of life.

But God listened to them all,
For many people prayed for mother,
For her to heal, for her to wake,
For me, Ruxandra and my father.
  He raised you up!

When Gina opened up her eyes,
Dan believed in Paradise,
And as happy as the god, Pan,
There was a kiss between them,
A to Brancusi, to Rodin
  A kiss of dreams.

Even now, I'm not even sure now which of us has really come back to life: she or I?

TO BE or TO HAVE?

They say that a wise man reached the outskirts of a village and laid under a tree for the night. A villager came running and shouted: "The rock! The rock! Give me the rock!" "What rock?" the wise man asked. "Last night, God came to me in my dream and said to me that if I go on the brink of the village at the twilight, an old man will give me a rock that will make me rich for the rest of my life."

The wise man took out a rock from his bag: "He must have meant this one. I found it yesterday in the woods. Well, take it if you want!" The man took the rock, not believing his eyes: it was the largest diamond in the world! After he came home, he turned and tossed in bed all night. In the morning, he went back to the wise man and said: "I changed my mind! Instead, give me that wealth that allowed you to hand over this rock to me without hesitation."

Oh, how fast did the villager catch on the true wealth! Because, in life, it does not matter what you have, but whom you have. Maybe your deluxe house is welcoming, but your soul is empty because you didn't know what to fill it with. Money can buy you a bed, but not sleep; you can buy yourself a position, but not respect; and you can buy sex, but not love! The clink of money is cold, but kind words are warm!

"You work like crazy all your life/ And you come to realize over the years / That you are poor the moment / When you lose souls, not money! / Life is a battle in which / We can call ourselves poor / When there are no voices / To ask 'How are you?'" Inspiring words, right?

So let us not educate ourselves to collect wealth, but rather to be happy because this is the way we will come to know the true value of things and not their price. We will realize what others already know: that the best days of our lives are not those when we have something, but the days when we have someone...

Chapter 7: Fulfillment

"Success is achieving everything you want. Happiness is wanting everything you've achieved."
Dale Carnegie

"A Zen master and his apprentice lived in a small village. When the apprentice turned 16, he received a horse as a gift, and all the villagers exclaimed: 'How wonderful!' The Zen master looked at them impassively and said, 'We shall see...'

After about two years, the apprentice fell off the horse and broke his leg, and all the villagers exclaimed, 'What a blow!' The Zen master looked at them impassively and said, 'We shall see...'

Not long after that, a war broke out, and all men in the village were drafted, except the apprentice, who was permanently injured. All the villagers exclaimed, 'How wonderful!' The Zen master looked at them impassively and said, 'We shall see...' "

This master was a wise man, wasn't he? Let me show you how this parable directly applied in my life.

One morning when I was three years old, my mother was cooking and put a pot of water on the stove. When the water started boiling, she realized she'd run out of burners, so she took the pot off the stove.

To prevent me from falling into it, she put it behind the kitchen door. Nevertheless, that's exactly what happened: I came into the house with a ball in my hands, and when I entered the kitchen, I kicked it and started running after it. The ball hit a table leg and bounced right behind the door. I ran after it, tripped, and fell hands-first into the scalding water!

Upon hearing about this accident, all the villagers exclaimed, "What a disaster!" If master Zen would have lived in Uioara de Sus, he certainly would have had a more impassive reaction: "We shall see."

Years later, when I was starting 8th form, an officer from the Military Secondary School in Alba-Iulia came to my school, recruiting potential candidates. I had excellent academic scores, was good at sports, and wanted to join the military. But no such luck. The scars on my hands from the burns were considered to be distinguishing marks, which were sufficient to exclude me from consideration.

While I was upset for couple of months because my access to a military career was blocked, today I feel that this unfortunate event placed a footprint on my destiny. When I told my mother how much I wanted to go to military school, she offered to make a huge sacrifice and overcome the physical deficit with a skin graft. Extremely surprised, I asked her, "Can doctors do that?" From that point on, my admiration for the medical profession became lodged in my subconscious, so when it came time to choose my career, medicine was a natural choice. So Zen master, you were right!

However, I've discovered that it doesn't work for me to pass through life like water off a duck's back – without being imbued by the vital passion that God granted me at birth. So I decided to try to be wiser than the Zen master: When something good happens to me, like the villagers, I exclaim: "How wonderful!"

And when something bad happens, I react, as impassively as the Zen master: "We shall see."

But I can't always pull it off. That's why my name isn't Master Dan!

The Rivers of Fulfillment

There are so many successful people, but they're not happy. Why is that? Maybe it's because they're always unsatisfied with what they've acquired. Or maybe it's because success is based on two qualities: earnestness and common sense. And if you don't have these qualities, your success is guaranteed!

I picture happiness as being a calm, incredibly turquoise sea, like the one that bathes the white sands of the Navagio beach on the island of Zakynthos. Just like any sea, it's formed by the inflow of certain rivers.

The first river is *family fulfillment*. The soul drinks from this river on a daily basis in an attempt to keep the serenity we strive throughout our entire lives. A life partner's warm and trustworthy smile, the joy in your children's eyes, your plans for the future, and beautiful memories are all like balm for the soul.

Leaving the house to face life, we all have moments when we feel as if we've entered a blizzard that relentlessly whips our cheeks and makes snowdrifts on the paths of our minds. But back home with the door closed behind us, we feel that snow melting. The roar of the blizzard disappears, the house is warm, and there is food for the soul on the table.

The river of *spiritual fulfillment* discharges a vast amount of water into the sea of happiness! Without a doubt, the "vertical dimension" is a priority. Then you'll know that Someone full of kindness and wisdom is beside you every second, that you can always count on His support, and that all the obstacles you trip over are only there so you'll feel His hands helping you up back on your feet. Blessed be God's name!

The "horizontal dimension" of spiritual fulfillment defines the quality of our relationship with ourselves. The inner dialogue we have in day-to-day life is a dialogue that comes in the shape of a Q&A. The more questions marks that stir up our consciousness, the more abrasive the inner dimensions.

To reveal the meaning of life, we really only need to have clear-cut answers to three essential questions: Who are we? Where did we come from? Where are we headed?

The answers to these questions will increase our chances of coming face-to-face with the greatest challenge in life: to discover who we really are. In the meantime, let us accept another one of life's challenges: to be happy with what we've discovered.

Some read to fall asleep, and others read to wake up. Someone once said that in five years' time we will be the same, except for the books we have read and the people we have met. So let's learn something new every day. But be careful: The door to personal advancement can only be opened from the inside.

In order to advance ourselves, we must interact with the people around us. And there are teachers everywhere. Wise men learn from others, smart people learn from their mistakes, and stupid people know it all. So let's never get to the point where we know it all!

The river of *professional fulfillment* has a flow that differs from one person to another. Some experience it as an essential pillar in their lives. They identify what defines them as professionals and what, from their perspective, validates them in society. Depending on this referencing and the congruence between expectation and achievement, we will either find ourselves before a person that is content or one that is tormented by their professional status.

The purity of the water in the river of *social fulfillment* depends on the quality of relationships we establish with the people around us. Day-to-day interactions, the way we feel validated, the way we present ourselves to the people we encounter, and the status we have achieved in society are all elements that either bring us contentment or inner struggles. Are we good to our fellow men? Remember, whatsoever a man sows, that shall he also reap!

Having a good heart in a world so cruel is courage, not weakness. The Dalai Lama said we should be amiable whenever possible. He added, "And that's always possible."

The river of *physical and mental health* is just as important. It seems you cannot enjoy anything if you aren't healthy, especially if it's a chronic or incurable disease. My sister-in-law is an exception. She's had a terrible health problem for many years, yet she still exudes an abundance of positive energy. It's as if she owns an optimism factory!

For most of us, illness feels like a burden on us, as well as those around us. It doesn't really matter if the illness afflicts the body or the mind. Psychiatrists say that one in four persons suffer from some kind of psychiatric disorder. So if you're together with three other friends and can't see anything strange in them, don't think about it anymore!

I remember my daughter Ruxandra once told me: "Daddy, I really care about your health because if there's no you, there can't be me."

If the five rivers of fulfillment flow smoothly, then they will create a sea of happiness.

Assessing Your Fulfillment

There is a very simple way to assess a man's happiness. It has been proven that a happy person has a faster pulse (accelerated by 4 beats per minute), smoother skin and eyes with an intense glow. But a truer measurement of happiness can be made with a needle and thread! Studies conducted on happy people have shown that even their fingers tend to tremble less. In other words, the faster you manage to pass a thread through a needle's eye, the more abundant happiness will be in your life!

Italian movie star Monica Vitti stated: "Some say this world belongs to the early riser. Wrong! This world belongs to happy people!" How do you assess happiness? Well, a smart person thinks that the one who is right is also happy. But a wise man knows that a happy person is right. Therefore, when you meet happy people, follow their guidance. It's worth it!

The Prince's Quest

"A king had a smart and courageous son. In order to prepare him to face life's hardships, he sent him to an old wise man.

'Enlighten me, 'the prince said to the old wise man. 'What do I need to know in life?'

'My words will be as lost on you as your footsteps in the sand,' said the wise man. 'But I will give you a piece of advice. On your road through life, you will get to three gates. Read all that is written on each of them. A desire more powerful than you will push you to follow their words. Don't try to retreat, or you will be damned to relive—again and again—all that you are trying to avoid. I cannot tell you more. You alone must go through this experience, with your heart and your body. Now go! Follow the path in front of you.'

The old wise man disappeared, and the young man set off down the path. Soon, he found himself standing before a large gate that said CHANGE THE WORLD. 'That was my intention, 'the prince said to himself. 'Even if there are things I like in this world, some don't sit well with me at all.'

Then his first battle began: His ideals, ability and vigor had pushed him to face the world – to engage and shape reality as he wished. He discovered the pleasure and arousal of conquering, but not the soothing of his heart. He managed to change a few things, but many others did not yield.

Years passed. One day, he met the old wise man again, who asked him, 'What did you learn on this path?'

'I learned to differentiate between the things that lie within my power and the things that escape me – what is up to me, and what isn't.'

'Good,' said the old man. 'Use your influence over what lies within your power, and forget about anything that slips through your fingers.' Having said that, the wise man once again disappeared.

After a while, the prince found himself before a second gate that said CHANGE OTHERS. 'That was my intention, 'he thought. 'Others are sources of pleasure, satisfaction and joy, but also of pain, hardship and frustration.' He thus raised his hand against anyone that annoyed him, and tried to forcefully remove their flaws.

While he was pondering the usefulness of his attempts to change others, he encountered the old wise man again, who asked him, 'What have you learned on this path?'

'I have learned that others are not the causes of joys or hardships, or of satisfactions or defeats. Rather, they occasionally bring them to the surface. All these things take root inside me.'

'You are right,' said the old man. 'With everything that others awaken inside you, they unravel something else before your eyes. Be grateful to those who make joy and pleasure vibrate inside you, as well as those that create suffering and frustration inside you. Through them, life shows you that there's still more to learn, and reveals the path you should follow.'

Not long afterward, the prince reached a third gate that said CHANGE YOURSELF. 'If I am the root of my own problems, then I need to do that,' he said to himself, and he started a battle against himself. He tried to reach inside himself and forcefully remove his own flaws – to change everything that did not match his ideal self. He had some success, but also some failure and resistance.

A few years later, the prince once again met the old wise man, who asked him, 'What have you learned on this path?'

'I have learned that there are things inside us that we can improve, and others that will not yield.'

'That's right,' the old man said.

'Yes, but I'm tired of fighting against everything and everyone, including myself! Does it ever end? I feel like giving up, giving in and letting go.'

'This will be your last lesson, but before going any further, turn back and contemplate the road you have travelled,' answered the old man. Then he disappeared.

Looking back at the other side of the third gate, the prince found that it said ACCEPT YOURSELF. He was amazed that he hadn't looked back and seen those words when he passed through it the first time. 'In battle, we become blind,' he said.

On the ground all around him, he saw everything he'd rejected and defeated during the battle he fought against himself: flaws, shadows, fears and limitations. He recognized them all, and he learned to accept and love them. Therefore, he learned to love himself, without making comparisons, judging, or blaming himself.

Then he met the old wise man again, who asked him,' What have you learned on this path that you didn't know before?'

'I have learned that I shouldn't hate any part of myself, even if it's not in alignment with who I want to be. In other words, I've learned to accept myself completely and unconditionally.'

'Good. This is the first thing you must never forget in life. Now you can go farther.'

In the distance, the prince saw the second gate again. The back of it said ACCEPT OTHERS. Around him, he recognized all the individuals he'd encountered: the ones he'd loved and the ones he'd hated, the ones he'd helped and the ones he'd battled. But to his surprise, he was now incapable of seeing their imperfections: the very things that had intensely annoyed him and that he'd fought against.

The old wise man appeared again and asked him, 'What have you learned on this path that you didn't know before?'

'When I'm properly aligned, I never want to reprimand others, and I'm no longer afraid of them. And I've learned to accept and love them the way they are.'

'Good. This is the second thing you must keep in mind.'

Then the prince saw the first gate in the distance, which he had first passed through so long ago. The back of it said ACCEPT THE WORLD. He looked around and recognized the world he'd wanted to conquer, convert and change. It hit him how bright and beautiful everything was: it was perfection. But it was still the same world as before. Did the world change, or did his perspective change?

Then the old man appeared and asked him, 'What have you learned on this path that you didn't know before?'

'That this world is the mirror of my soul. That I don't see the world, but I see myself in it. When I am happy, the world seems wonderful. When I am in low spirits, the world seems sad. In truth, it is neither joyful nor sad. It just is. It wasn't the world that bothered me, but my state of mind and the worries I had. I have learned to accept it without judging it, without conditions.'

'This is the third important thing you must not forget. Now you are at peace with yourself, with the others, and with the world! You are ready to set off towards your last challenge: passing from the quietness of fulfillment, to the fulfillment of quietness,' the wise man said. Then he disappeared forever."

We learn something new every day—from the moment we wake up until the moment we collapse in bed at night, exhausted. We learn from others and from our own mistakes. We usually assimilate the lesson on the first try, but sometimes, we need to repeat it several times until we learn it by heart because we cannot believe the same lesson applies to several circumstances. We should know that *a repeated mistake is no longer a mistake, but a choice.*

But sometimes, we have no idea what lesson we are supposed to learn from what's happening to others. We may also need time to discover the true purpose of our experiences. All we have to do is be patient. We'll find the meaning of the lesson at some point! But could we find it too late? Well, that is another matter...

Chapter 8: Balance

"We all have two lives; the second starts when we realize there's only one."
Confucius

They say one cannot do anything about the length of their life, but you can certainly do something about its depth. So "dig, brother, dig, dig until you see stars in the water," as Lucian Blaga advised. If you are not an amateur for physical labor, you have the alternative of thought, so there is a chance to alter the limits of your life – some say life is too short for those who think, and it's too long for those who don't think.

A nurse working in a palliative care hospital granted to patients in terminal stages of a disease thought of publishing a book with the most common regrets of man found before death. At the top, there is the regret of having worked too much, thus missing precious time that could have been spent with their family and friends. It's possible the following joke was inspired by reality: "The wife said to the husband: 'See the little boy in this picture?' 'Yes, I see him,' the husband answered. 'At 5 o'clock this afternoon, go to the kindergarten and bring him home, understood?' "

Oh, I'm so silly! I offer jokes as part of my argument, but I forget about the confession of a friend who was very busy with varied business affairs and who shared: "Today, when I got home, my wife threw a fit at me, screaming and shouting that our son, aged 5, is not actually mine! I was devastated! After she calmed down a bit, she told me that next time I should pay more attention to whom I pick up and bring home from the kindergarten." So we should pay more attention to other people's mishaps, so that we don't repeat them!

You Cannot Shake Hands with a Clenched Fist

As I am writing these pages, there are numerous anti-government protests taking place in Romania. Activists are fighting against an emergency ordinance that, at a first glance, would benefit a group of powerful individuals with legal problems. Since this political act has been sanctioned by public opinion and international bodies, I was surprised by the intensity of the two opposing sides. It's as if demons hibernating for years have awoken, and they want to make up for lost time.

The internet is loaded with rather trenchant opinions and attitudes. Toxic words pour out against opposing parties. Flags are waved, and revolutions are rumored. Otherwise honorable individuals incessantly bark and post pestilential slander. While indulging in this hornets' nest, lifelong friendships disappear as if they never existed.

There is constant talk about people being manipulated. Given the high stakes, it's hard for me to think it's not likely. I won't get into the details, but I will reference a well-known maxim: Toujour cherchez l'argent! (Always look for the money!) Of course, my opinion will upset the protesters, especially since many of them are intellectuals with remarkable IQs.

In fact, I don't know anyone who would easily accept the idea of being manipulated. Let's not forget the pedestals on which we place our opinions, and our innate refusal to accept the idea of being controlled by someone else. Try recalling how often you've heard phrases such as:

- "You were right!"
- "I was wrong!"
- "Please forgive me!"

Not very often, right?

I believe that those who are now protesting in the name of heightened principles are losing sight of an essential element: "The Real Romania." Let me give you an example of what The Real Romania means to me.

A few days ago, I admitted an 80-year-old woman suffering from pneumonia into my clinic. I asked her about her living situation, and her answer moved me deeply: "Doctor, I live with my son and my 8-year-old grandson, because his mother went to Italy on business, and never came back. All winter, we slept in one room without a fire because we had no money to buy wood. And when we were finally able to get the wood, we preferred to warm the room where my grandson sleeps." She stretched out her trembling, labored hands and sighed: "My hands and feet were so cold!"

My dears, we should be protesting for this Romania! Many Romanians just like this grandmother aren't able to keep warm, and budgeting more for the pitiful pensions of these people could prevent this kind of problem. In fact, 100 lei can make the difference between good health and a serious disease, or even death! Those who pound their fists on their chests and haughtily state that the government can't buy them with 100 lei should donate this amount to their elders! Or better yet, they could ask their parents or grandparents if they could use some alms from the government. My parents could certainly use some!

Romania isn't like Sweden. About 20 years ago, their Parliament had an intense discussion about whether it was moral to cut off the tails of dogs!

I wondered why Romanians didn't start protesting seven years ago, when wages and pensions were being cut. At that time, people died because hospitals were being closed down, but politicians in power were still filling up their pockets. Since these same politicians are now being called thieves, the true civic conscience of today's protesters should be equal to the attitude back then.

Why are they protesting now, but weren't a few years ago? For a large percentage of them, the difference in their positions probably has a lot to do with the motivations of selfies and likes. "Protests are fashionable, so let's go to one of them. Then we'll have something to post on Facebook this evening!"

To stress their determination to fight against the government, these protestors use this slogan: "I resist!" But there's a huge difference between that kind of resistance and the resistance you can see in the eyes of our elders. So many times, they look so tired of illness (and of life) that you can almost hear them thinking: "I feel like I'm the only one who still knows how to resist..."

So the time has come to:

- Unclench our hateful fists.
- Free ourselves from irrational political passions.
- Keep our political convictions in check.
- Hug one another before we protest.
- Embrace our authentic values, realizing that we're too small for such a big war, and that our decisions are still unfortunately made by other parties.

We truly need for heartfelt Romanians to join hands, rather than tearing each other apart—before it's too late.

Raise Your Value, Not Your Voice

"A wise man in India asked his disciples why people shout when they're upset.

'We shout because we lose our temper,' one of them answered. 'But why shout if the other person is right next to you?'

'Well, we shout to make sure the other person hears us,' another one explained. 'Still, isn't it possible to speak in a lower voice?'

None of the answers satisfied the wise man. Then he explained it to them:

'When two people argue, their hearts distance themselves from each other. In order to cover this distance, they must shout to hear one other. The angrier they are, the more they feel they must shout because of the ever-growing distance between their hearts. However, what happens when two people are in love? They don't scream at all; they whisper. Why? Because their hearts are very close to one another. Sometimes, their hearts are so close that they don't even speak at all; they just whisper and hum. And when their love is even more intense, there is no need for them to even whisper. It's enough to just look at each other, and their hearts communicate. So during a dispute, don't allow your hearts to become separated from one another, because there will come a day when the distance will be so large that your hearts won't be able to find their way back.' "

Gandhi assessed this musing as follows: "If you scream, everybody will hear you. If you whisper, only the one that's next to you will hear you. If you are silent, only the one who loves you will hear you."

I don't think there is one man on earth who has never shouted. Even Jesus, the epitome of kindness, shouted at the Pharisees who had turned God's temple into a marketplace. But He may be the only one who never regretted the tone He used. The rest of us all have moments when we regretted not being able to keep our tempers in check. Even more unfortunate, those we burn with the scorching flames of our verbal outbursts may not be the ones responsible for the lava boiling inside us. We charge ourselves with negative energies, and unload them on innocent people— essentially turning them into Pompeii, and covering their souls in ashes.

Studies say that screaming plays a beneficial role in the body, because it releases negative energies such as stress. *You know what stress is, right? It's waking up, screaming, then finding out you aren't actually sleeping.*

We are all aware of the negative effects that stress has on our bodies. First of all, there are cardiovascular problems, but also psychiatric and digestive problems. So avoiding stress should be one of our daily concerns.

But this focus obviously isn't an invitation to scream at people, just because it releases built-up tension inside. A more convenient variant would be to go to the outskirts of town and scream at the top of your lungs until you cool down, then rejoin your dear ones, smiling. In the end, the rain—not the thunder—helps the grass grow...

Don't Be Too Sweet or Bitter

If you're overly sweet, they'll eat you up. But if you're too bitter, they'll spit you out!

The adage above urges moderation in our many attempts to find our place in the universe. Networking is twice conditioned—by both ourselves and those we come into contact with. So it becomes essential to consider both entities. Too much bragging will certainly generate envy; too little will lead to indifference. Ideally, all of our actions will have the right balance.

Humankind is God's creation, which can be seen in the smallest details of design. And in connection with this concept, I will refer to how taste is perceived. Sweet taste receptors are located at the tip of the tongue, whereas bitter taste receptors are at the back of the tongue.

Do you think this situation occurred by accident? Humanity is a variable blend of bitterness and sweetness. An interaction between two individuals who don't know each other activates instinctively the innate reflex by which they discovered the world when they were infants: Everything that was new needed to be tasted. It's true that each time we try to make a good impression on those around us, we strive to decant our personality and offer a sip or two of it to others.

Two chemistry teachers have told me that bitterness in humans has a higher molecular weight than sweetness, so it will be the first to settle down. Naturally, people around us will taste our sweetness first, as there are more sweet taste receptors on the tips of our tongues. While the tongue has some bitter impurities, they won't be felt at first, since the bitter taste receptors are at the back of the tongue.

Issues occur with those who love and cherish us since they come to us thirsty all the time. They want to drink up our personality, and they'll reach the bottom of the bottle at some point, where the bitterness settles. Naturally, we'll have to offer them these bitter bits as well, even though the taste is so intense that we'll sometimes spit it out.

To me, here's the takeaway from this train of thought: Do you want to admire a person? Look up to them from afar. Do you want to know a person? Look at them closely. In the end, in matters of taste, there can be no dispute; taste is to be enjoyed, not discussed!

People who are in love are very specific. I, for one, believe that lovers simply no longer feel the bitter taste, due to the chemistry between them. This phenomenon also accounts for a sudden change of bitter taste receptors into sweet taste receptors. This is also the reason for an unquenchable drinking from all the blend of qualities and flaws in their loved one. Studies have concluded that the metamorphosis of this receptor disappears after three years, so the bitter taste can be perceived again.

You may not know this, but the term honeymoon was originally used to indicate the period of time (a moon cycle) when a newlywed couple would drink mead (a honey-based aphrodisiac). In Eastern Europe, a honeymoon is still sometimes called a honey month. So after three years, the lovers are usually connected by both love and a sheet of paper called a marriage license. Today, we have a joke in Romania: After the sometimes-dreaded sheet of paper is moistened in honey for a month, you are no longer swallowed, nor spit out; you are chewed like chewing gum!

Control Your Lips

While the thought of being drunk on love may be alluring, loose lips sink ships.

So remember this: If you want to assess a man's wisdom, measure the words that come out of his mouth. And if you want to assess his soul, measure the sincerity of his smile.

A man's IQ level and wisdom are directly proportionate to the collaboration of his brain, his vocal cords, and the orbicular muscle in his mouth (the one that puckers the lips when it contracts). While there is an excellent connection between grey matter and vocal cords in the intelligent man, the same cannot be applied to the muscle mentioned above, which usually does not manage to contract itself efficiently. Therefore, it doesn't automatically screen the thoughts that reach the outside world. A wise man is the one who holds the ability to master the orbicular muscle around his mouth. He will not say everything he thinks, but he will think about everything he says.

As W.L. Wilmhurst said, *"Control your lips, for they are the gates to the palace, and the king resides inside."*

Contrasts

As they say, the truth lies somewhere in the middle. But it would be so sad if the truth was there all the time, because then mediocre endeavors would result in genius outcomes (to paraphrase Lucian Blaga). Likewise, we can be safeguarded from useless torment by applying moderation to appraisals, and serenely accepting that we cannot always be right.[5]

The Herald may stand for the impossibility of the common man to understand the drama of the artist, for the incapacity of a mediocre person to assimilate the aspirations of the genius.

---

[5] Lucian Blaga was a Romanian philosopher, poet, playwright, and novelist.

So many times along our life path, we will be surprised by the type of reality that Romanian poet Virgil Carianopol masterfully depicted in his piece "Contrasts":

There are joys that sadden us.
There is sadness that makes us happy.
There are days without light
And deep nights that are bright.
There are truths that put us down,
And there are lies that lift us up.
There are omnipotent emperors
Who tremble in fear.
There are sweets that taste as bitter as bile,
And there is bitterness that tastes like sugar.
There is injustice that puts things straight.
There is justice that is unjust...

An Eye for an Eye

In the Old Testament, "an eye for an eye, a tooth for a tooth" was as a practical expression of the law of retaliation. It was a variant of criminal justice falling somewhere between revenge and the fair reciprocity of crime and punishment. It seemed natural, logical and legal to the people at that time, so it was practiced without making too many amendments.

But then Jesus' arrival radically changed the meaning of this custom, advocating that you should turn the other cheek if someone hits you. In this moment, Jesus was making an extreme point to demonstrate how out of control "an eye for an eye" had gotten, but He wasn't expecting to be taken literally two thousand years later, yet contemporary fundamentalists still do. Like never-ending penitence, a literal interpretation of this statement can be very counterproductive, even masochistic. While we should follow Jesus' example, we shouldn't be martyrs at the expense of our health or the advancement of society.

As Nicolae Iorga said, "Be good, but beware: do not let the world think that you can be only good!" Why? Well, because you risk being taken advantage of! One of my dear friends used to frequently call me a "good man." While I value people calling me this, I have to prove that I could be not only a good man. So every three months or so, I go to the nurses' office, and I slam my fist on the table! Of course, this startles all the nurses, who often ask: "What happened, doctor?" "Nothing, my dears! I just wanted you to see that I'm capable of having this reaction."[6]

It's true: The temptation to make a fool out of someone else can be downright irresistible, as long as, when you concede to others they can take advantage of you. "Let him go, let him carry the weight if he's a wooden head!" We all have been classified as such many times throughout life. Many times we were not aware of it at all. But there were also situations in which we really weren't martyrs, but just good people, taking on the full burden of a certain job. In those moments, we weren't afraid of being taken advantage of; we were only fearing God. And this is the only fear can be beneficial, if kept in balance.

---

[6]Nicolae Iorga was a Romanian historian, politician, literary critic, memoirist, poet, and playwright.

So I say: *we should load our arms with flowers and throw them to those who throw stones at us on the dusty road of life. If the flower is a potted flower...well, shit happens!*

The Math Quiz of Life

When trying to balance your life, remember that life is like taking a math quiz: We add up the joys and sad moments. We subtract ourselves in the eyes of some. We multiply the good or the bad that we receive. We divide our friends. And we make mistakes. When we realize we have made a mistake, we would like to erase it with a rubber eraser, but it leaves even darker marks. We would like to ask for another chance to start all over again, but sometimes there's no time, because the bell rings...

The Secret of Juggling

A few years back, Brian Dyson, the president of Coca-Cola, delivered a speech at a university on the connection between work and other responsibilities in life:

"Imagine life as a game in which you are juggling five balls in the air. You name them work, family, health, friends and spirit, and you're keeping all of these in the air. You will soon understand that work is a rubber ball. If you drop it, it will bounce back. But the other four balls – family, health, friends and spirit – are made of glass. If you drop one of these, they will be irrevocably scuffed, marked, nicked, damaged or even shattered. They will never be the same. You must understand that and strive for balance in your life."

This analogy is brilliant! I don't believe that anyone else has managed to capture the essence of this truth in such an insightful way. But to tell the truth, most people aren't workaholics, so they have careers to maintain their families, relationships, health and spirit. And yes, it's not that easy to balance them all. In fact, I think it's impossible to consistently manage them throughout life.

We will always prioritize one of the five balls, and I have a hunch that we almost always start with work. And if our efforts are financially successful, then we'll have enough time to enjoy the other parts of our lives. But mark my words: *It's better to have a beer belly than a hump on your back from working too hard!*

However we decide to live, it is essential to be aware that we only have one life – and if we live it well, that's enough.

Chapter 9: Integrity

"Worry more about your conscience than your reputation. Because your conscience is what you are; your reputation is what others think of you. And what others think of you is their problem"
Charlie Chaplin

Two years ago, I ran for Senate at Lucian Blaga University, which is the group that administrates the management of the school. I approached some colleagues, who were also interested in entering this management forum. After I didn't receive the majority of needed votes in the first two rounds, I learned that a colleague who'd agreed to offer mutual support had betrayed me. I promoted his name for both of those rounds until he was elected into the Senate. But when I found out that he'd benefited from the help of my adversary in exchange for some votes, I was stupefied!

As I expressed my surprise and disappointment for this kind of attitude, another nominee suggested: "What's the big deal? Go ahead and say that you'll support anyone who offers to support you, even if they compete against each another. That's how it's done, Dan!"

Maybe some people win this way, but I didn't. I had five requests to support the Dean of Law Faculty, but those who approached me about it responded by saying: "Send all my consideration to the dean, but I'm supporting his adversary from the first round. So he'll have to seek support somewhere else!'

As I related these events to my friend over the phone, I said: "Even my little daughter knows how to react in such a situation! Ruxandra, tell my friend how to manage a competition." I handed the phone to her, and without hesitation, she reiterated: "Better to fail than cheat!"

I was finally elected via supplementary motions in the third round. According to a friend from the vice-chancellor's office, I was "the talk of the university" for three full rounds. Even though it took me a little longer, I was elected to the Senate – fair and square. So work on your reputation, and your reputation will work for you. And seek to attract respect, not attention – it lasts longer!

Zero or Hero

A famous mathematician in the Middle Ages was asked to give a definition of man from a mathematical angle. His answer was brilliant: *"If the man is of character and shows common sense, that is equal to one. If he's also handsome, he's equal to ten. If he's also rich, he's equal to a hundred. If he's a nobleman, a thousand. But if his character and common sense disappear, he has only zeroes."*

We all meet so many zeros throughout our lives. Starting in childhood, our attention is drawn to the fact that we will often encounter evil and indifference. But it still seems like none of us are ready for the reality that we find ourselves in: A few ones floating in an ocean of zeroes. When I was a teenager, if I'd thought that I'd only meet a single one for every 10 zeroes, I would have been very disillusioned.

Of course, in the end, a zero has its purpose in the world: Everything around us is a binary system. In order to see the Power of One, ones must be surrounded by zeroes! But quite often, we've all born witness to an assault of zeroes against a one, in a natural attempt to take his/her place. You remember the frustration you experienced when you saw the satisfied smile of a zero who'd taken the place of a one, correct?

Constantin Brancusi, a Romanian sculptor and painter, said that most people see the world like a fatal pyramid, which they crowd inside to get as close to the top as possible. For this reason, they often step on each other and rip and tear one another, and end up completely unhappy. Meanwhile, if they grew and fulfilled themselves in a natural manner, they could rely on their own character and common sense in all of life's circumstances.

Hot Confidence

Those who have climbed up on top of a pile of books to look at God and to get breathe the hard air of high altitudes have a different perspective of the world. Instead of becoming dizzy from the rarefied air, they have a better foothold on their lives and anchor their heads more securely on their shoulders.

While they're standing at this altitude, their soul is intertwined with others. Instead of imposing things, they assert themselves. Instead of shining, they prefer to warm others. Their steps don't leave dust on the road of life, so that those who follow them won't lose sight of them. These individuals know they're wise men.

If we really want something, we'll find a way; if not, we'll find some excuse. A variety of areas of life, including success as a doctor or an author, necessitates one's capacity to attract others' attention to you without being pompous or ostentatious. In this respect, self-promotion is a sine qua non.

However, some seek the limelight like fireflies. They ignore the reality that ostentation can be one of the most despised flaws in a person, and the reason is very simple: their firefly personalities invade our intimate spaces by causing hypertrophy, which results in us turning our backs on them. Ultimately, this makes an arrogant person seem like a balloon; he puffs himself up, but he's empty inside.

So remember: confidence is HOT, but arrogance is NOT!

Untainted

It's not easy to keep one's character and common sense untainted in today's world. The pressures are high. Many times, life seems like a crazy race, but it's important to remember you're not running it alone. Some of your opponents may resort to dirty maneuvers to create advantages for themselves. These types of people didn't enter the ranks fairly; they sneaked in.

You've probably heard someone say, "*The more you get to know people, and the more people you get to know, the more you understand why Noah only put animals in his Ark.*" This quote most likely refers to those previously mentioned individuals.

For people with character and common sense, many circumstances will test their integrity throughout their lives. These people schedule their races in a manner that will not affect their integrity. After all, it is their most important trait, the one that allows them to maintain their values. That's why you'll often see them walking on the side of the road, contemplating all the hustle and bustle around them. As the famous Romanian song about the ripe tree and the good fellow says, good people often prefer to overlook the mistakes of the people around them, so they can continue being kind to them.

But it can be hard to keep yourself unruffled after seeing others use their cheekiness, callousness and twisted ethics to cheat at the start of the race or to find shortcuts to get ahead of you. You get frustrated, and whether you want to or not, you're sometimes tempted to give up on the integrity that allows you to look at yourself in the mirror with dignity. You know that feeling, right?

The Role of Macrophages

Of course, in order to keep the physical integrity of His creation intact, God needed to implement a special defense mechanism. The cells that stay at the borders of the human body and guard against intruders are called macrophages. When they identify a foreign body, they process and destroy it. In order to accomplish this task, they collaborate with Memory B cells, which recognize the aggressor is making a new attempt to penetrate the body. Together, they synthesize rapid antibodies.

In some diseases, the number of macrophages is low, or their immunocompetence is compromised. Therefore, the body will be exposed to various, infectious offenders that will damage its physical integrity.

I recently had a revelation: The protective role of macrophages might not be limited to the physical body. Throughout our lives, we face various experiences that are potentially antigenic, such as lying, wickedness, betrayal and envy. It has clearly been proven that the chronic accumulation of negative energies leads to a depressive state, during which the immune system suffers from varying degrees of "paralysis." During these times, the body is more susceptible to infections.

Similarly, sick macrophages alter the proper functioning of Memory B cells, which are starting "to forget" that the previously mentioned vices aren't part of humankind's structure as it was created by God. As a result, they are incorporated into our beings and alter both our physical and personal integrity. I'll admit, it takes a lot of research to prove this theory!

The Most Valuable Trait

Your word is more valuable than your bank account. In fact, integrity is the most important human value, because it represents all your other good traits. It gives you the certainty of keeping them, regardless of the situation. Because of integrity, you never have to give up your values by repositioning yourself in relation to others, just because it would be more suitable for you.

Therefore, the consistency that defines your attitudes can easily be anticipated by those who know you. It's very important for others to trust what you say, and to not go back on your word.

Cutting Corners

I'll admit it: I wear a lot of hats. Not only am I an M.D. and professor, I also manage a medical center. Through my various experiences, I've observed that start-ups aren't easy to manage. Nowadays, it's definitely difficult to start a business that will provide for you and your family, and it's even harder to achieve a balance between work and family. Until you get it off the ground, the consumption of physical, psychological and time resources can dampen the inspiration of entrepreneurs. In order to move through this stage, you will sometimes be tempted to send your conscience to sleep and can cut corners, so you can get ahead. I think this is how author Ambroise Bierce reached this definition of a pocket: "the cradle of wishes and the tomb of conscience."

The Empty Cart

"One morning, a boy was walking in the woods with his father. At one point, the man stopped and listened for a few seconds.

Then he asked his son: 'Besides the rustling of leaves and the birds singing, what else can you hear?'

'I can hear a cart, father!'

'That is true,' the father answered. 'More than that, it's an empty cart.'

'How do you know it's empty if we can't see it yet?'

'That's simple: by the noise it makes. The emptier a cart is, the noisier it gets.' "

In day-to-day life, when we see a person speaking too much, interrupting everybody else's conversations, being intrusive and infatuated, or feeling high and mighty and belittling those around him, we should remember this father's observation.

Most people think that being a show-off is an annoying character flaw. No matter what you try to highlight about yourself, the more you toot your own horn—be it for some talent or some achievement—the less you impress your audience.

It's really an art to know how to invade the space of those you interact with without being perceived as an antigen structure whose purpose is to sabotage them. Their immune system will automatically be enabled, so they will do everything in their power to eliminate you from their surroundings as soon as possible. Moreover, just like Memory B cells, your aggressor-type image will be remembered for a long time, having been reactivated each and every time you're around them – even if your attitude no longer has warlike tendencies, and you've become the most unpretentious person in the world.

Psychological warfare can conquer vast territories without bloodshed. If logical intelligence attracts admiration, emotional intelligence brings about sympathy and success. It's the trait that allows us to reach down to the heart of our enemies without creating significant disturbances in its electrical activity. They say that a direct approach is the fastest way to many troubles. Well, emotional intelligence uses workarounds that create short circuits, avoiding the reflex mechanism of defense of other people, which can swiftly trigger and instantly sabotage any attempt to advance toward them.

Still waters run deep. Moderation, kindness and common sense were traits of Jesus, Gandhi, Mother Theresa, and Pope John Paul II. Their passage through the world did not involve inconveniently splashing those around them; instead it was through calmly and organically filling others' souls with peace.

However, it's important to keep in mind that Jesus was nothing short of a PR genius. By all means, sell yourself, but do it with modesty. That way, people will want to help you succeed, rather than shoot you down because they view you as a braggart.

Triumphant Authenticity

Ultimately, your conscience follows you through every step of your life. And yes, you can never detach yourself from it, unless you develop some sort of schizoid disorder. At that point, you might say something like this: "I have a split personality, and I'm developing a third!"

Outside of this kind of situation, you'll have to be accountable to your conscience for your attitude each day.

Throughout my life, I've met a variety of characters who have acted unscrupulously in numerous circumstances and had a negative impact on those around them. Nevertheless, their faces appeared to be peaceful and carefree. So regarding integrity, I'm not talking about the kind of people whose consciences are sublime, but completely lacking (as Ion Luca Caragiale once humorously said). Rather, I'm talking about people who value good ethics. Eventually, some kind of cyanosis of their moral values will alter the peaceful flow of their lives. That kind of situation creates turbulence by corrupting the clear waters of the soul.[7]

Having good character will allow you to triumph over your own faults and others' schemes, so you'll have a peaceful conscience and a stronger reputation. But it all starts from the inside. To truly persuade others, you must be authentic, and avoid the kind of cheap roguery that some use to gain advantages over others.

You can always fool some people, and sometimes you can fool everyone. But you cannot always fool everyone!

Distorted Reflection

It's a great thing to be able to look at yourself in the mirror and be content with what you see. If the reflection is distorted for some reason, cleaning the mirror will be futile. You must correct the cause of the distortion. Otherwise, you'll only be able to attain

---

[7]Ion Luca Caragiale was a Romanian playwright, short story writer, poet, political commentator, and journalist.

a golden gloss that will create a bleak impression of the man you really are. You'll be similar to the apple the evil queen offered to Snow White: it makes the mouth water, but it poisons the soul.

The Seed of Integrity

"The general manager of a company realized he would need to name his replacement before he retired, so he called a meeting with the entire management team and announced:

'In exactly one year, I will appoint a successor as the general manager of the company. Today, I intend to give each of you a special seed. I want you to take it home with you, plant it and water it. Then in exactly one year, come back to me with the plant that has grown from that seed. On that day, I will analyze your plant, and based on personal criterion, I'll choose the next general manager.'

A young man named Jim was present at the meeting. Like all of his colleagues, he received a seed. He went home and excitedly shared his boss's plan with his wife. She helped him find a suitable pot and top-quality earth enriched with natural fertilizer. Each day, Jim would water the soil and eagerly waited for any sign that the seed had sprouted and a small plant had emerged.

After three weeks, his colleagues were talking about their plants, which had started growing. Jim closely watched the pot, but nothing changed. A month passed, and the pot showed no sign of sprouting or growing. His colleagues were already talking about their plants, and Jim felt like he'd failed. Six weeks passed, and nothing changed in Jim's pot.

Extremely disappointed, he realized he'd somehow killed the seed. Each of his colleagues already had large plants, but the only thing he had was soil. Nevertheless, Jim decided to keep watering his seed but not to tell his colleagues anything about his failure. Maybe it would sprout at some point.

After a year, each of the employees who had received a seed were sent a memo about a meeting during which the boss would inspect their plants. That night, Jim told his wife he dared not go to the meeting with an empty pot. But she encouraged him to be honest about what happened. Although he had a nervous feeling in his stomach thinking about how embarrassed he would be, he still decided listened to his wife.

When Jim entered the conference room for the meeting, he was shocked at the variety of plants his colleagues had. The plants were all different sizes and colors, but they all looked wonderful. When Jim's colleagues saw his plant-less pot, many of them burst out laughing, and some actually felt sorry for him. So by the time the boss came in, Jim was hiding in a corner.

'Wow, what beautiful plants you've grown!' The boss proclaimed. 'Today, one of you will be appointed as the company's general manager.'

All of a sudden, the boss discovered Jim in the corner and called him forward. Jim froze. He thought, 'The boss has seen my failure. I'll be lucky if he doesn't sack me.' Nevertheless, he told the boss his story.

When Jim finished, the boss asked them all to sit down, everyone except for Jim. Then pointing at him, the boss said: 'This is your new general manager!'

Everyone was dumbfounded, and Jim couldn't believe his ears! How could he be named the general manager after such a failure?

The boss explained: 'A year ago, I gave each of you a seed. What you didn't know is that all the seeds I gave you…had been boiled, so they were all dead and couldn't sprout anything. But everyone except Jim brought me full-grown plants. When you realized that the seed I've given you wouldn't sprout, you replaced it with one you bought. Jim was the only one who had the honesty and courage to bring back the vessel with my seed in it. That's why he'll be appointed the new general manager!' "

Honesty and courage are the two of the most important traits you can have. People who consistently nurture them will certainly emerge as winners. They might not win in all areas, since there are situations when giving up these values would create consistent advantages.

Therefore, they might find themselves in intensely doubtful circumstances. In these moments, cowardice and dishonesty haunt them with their warm embraces, which underlines the importance of immediate reward. In exchange, such acceptance often results in staring back at a cold reflection each and every time one looks at themselves in the mirror. But if they know how to cherish their values, they'll resist the temptation to give in to their internal pettiness.

In the long run, the benefits will be irrefutable. When you meet such people, try to keep them nearby.

It's extremely important to associate yourselves with people who share your values, not just your common interests.

Chapter 10: Assumptions

"Feelings buried alive never die."
Romanian Expression

Have you known someone who was suddenly, unexpectedly dumped by his girlfriend? Those feelings can linger indefinitely if he's still in love with her when she breaks up with him.

For instance, I sent one of my friends the following message one day: "Do you remember the day when someone plucked the sun from the sky and placed it in your soul?"

He answered, "Oh, what have you just done to me, man? The memories you've evoked. Why can't I ever forget her?"

When I asked him about it, he confessed, "I can't stop thinking about her!" He'd recently ended his marriage, which had lasted for nearly 21 years. They'd had issues from the very beginning, but even when their feelings for each other further soured, they decided to stay together for their two children. You know what they say: "The chain of marriage is so heavy that sometimes it takes three people to carry it!"

In the midst of this emotional emptiness, my friend met the one who was to become the love of his life. She was an outstanding woman on every level, and she accepted his status as a married man for almost three years. But it was soon too much for her to continue in a relationship that didn't seem like it would ever have a happy ending. She abruptly broke up with him, leaving his soul to writhe in a tomb of loneliness.

"Nineteen years have passed since I met her, and not one day goes by that I don't think about her," my friend sighed. I replied, "When you can't remove someone from your mind and soul, it means that's where they're supposed to be. To enter someone's heart is a feat. To get out of it without hurting them is a work of art. And to stay there for life is a masterpiece!"

Unfortunately, some people constantly regret the "good one that got away" and can't see that some things simply weren't meant to be. And more importantly, they can't see the opportunity right in front of them through their fog of regret.

These souls don't allow the sun to shine on them because they are too busy sighing. They know that there is no good in a farewell, but there will be a time when sighing must stop, because in the end, only three things matter:

- How much you loved what was dear to you.
- How beautifully you lived your life.
- How elegantly you left behind everything that wasn't meant for you.

Inner Turmoil

Voltaire said that the hardest battle is the one you fight with yourself because you are on both sides.

Everyone has had at least one inner battle in their lifetime, a battle that kneads their soul like dough—because the difficulty of the struggle is derived from an instinctive desire to avoid the wounds of the heart. If the mind always knows what to do to calm down, well, the challenge resides in settling the soul down! The world around it is warm, sometimes down-right hot. Scalding steam penetrates it like a steak in the oven, and the chances it will roast are high. You try to protect your soul, to keep it safe from suffering. But remember, *you can't have a rainbow without a little rain.*

We will wage many battles throughout the years, and they usually end up tearing us apart. We can certainly turn a blind eye to things we don't want to see because that's what our brain commands us to do, but we cannot close our hearts to things we wish we didn't feel.

Yes, there are important moments in life when we side with our souls and don't factor in practicality. And there are decisive moments when we choose rationally, then regret it from the bottoms of our hearts. You've had them, and I've had them. That's why I think the most important factor in achieving peace of mind is not letting regret affect your decision-making.

Shadow Friends

Many people pass through our lives. Our gazes are drawn to them only to the extent that they incite our senses and thoughts. Then, we keep moving forward, smiling as a sign of gratitude for the beauty they brought into our lives. Or we can invite them to walk along beside us down our roads. Or we can completely change our own direction by following them on their path.

We may lose sight of some of these friends, but we gain others for life. We share everything with these people, from our trivial thoughts to our big dreams. One day, skimming through our photo albums, our children will ask us, "Who are these people?" And we will answer, with a little dyspnea of our soul: "They're people I spent the best days of my life with!"

There are many reasons why some friends remain silent. And there are circumstances when we might not understand their detachment. *But sometimes, we have no choice but to continue our journey without some people. If there is a place for them in our lives, they will catch up with us.*

The Importance of Reevaluation

Did you know that 99% of people who throw themselves from tall buildings change their mind before they touch the ground?

In life, some problems fall into categories that make us feel like there is only one option. Shades of grey are no longer accepted; everything has to be black or white. Many times, these decisions starve our beings; by definition, they entail giving up a part of ourselves. These decisions can change our lives. Whether we carefully weighed all sides of an issue or made a quick decision that was heavily influenced by intense emotions, we are so certain we made the right decision that we "wipe the dust off our feet," as the gospel of Luke said.

110

Time and again, life will prove that we were wrong to build walls, rather than leave a small door open to the past. And when I say that, I'm mainly thinking of the people we leave behind. In the end, I think there are many more elements that will lead us to this same conclusion.

First of all, a decision that may have fit like a glove at one point could feel like a spasm of the soul later on, after we've experienced some changes. Because life invariably changes, some undergo radical changes, but others are subjected to subtle ones. Moreover, pride often impedes us from reconsidering our decisions because that would mean admitting we were wrong.

Secondly, someone we decided to banish from our universe could feel the same way. They may regret wronging us, but not knowing whether we'd take them back, they dare not search for us. In other words, we may have to leave many people behind along the way, but we shouldn't burn bridges. We will be surprised by how many times, in our life, we will have to cross back over that river. So be careful about making radical decisions, especially if they're made spontaneously. If you dive in too hastily, you could suffer for a long time because of it.

Regret-Free Life

Never regret the past. Be glad it happened!

I think one of the most catabolically negative human emotions is regret. They may take the shape of this question: "Why did I act like that?" Or on the contrary, "Why didn't I do something?" Regardless, regrets are underpinned by the certainty that the option we opted against would have been better.

The human mind is built to regularly sabotage us by plotting positive scenarios as certain alternatives to our wrong choices, without factoring in a possibility that something even worse could have occurred if we had made a different choice. Based on my own experience, as well as on the experiences of some friends of mine, I do consider that the intensity of our regrets is higher if we preferred the paralysis of our actions instead of a hyperactivity which may lead to wounds.

In other words, when we look back on our lives, we may wonder, "How was I able to do that?" That option is better than sighing with nostalgia and asking, "Oh, how I wish I'd done that!" This related advice is also important: *Never regret anything you did if you were happy at that moment in time!*

Flood-Damaged Memories

I hope you can relate to the familiarity of having known people we've associated with pleasant memories and who can suddenly become a *persona non grata*. Almost instantly, everything we used to view as being precious about that person is seen in a different light. A flickering flame of good memories is extinguished by a solitary secret discovered posthumously. The door to the room in the soul where we gather dear memories slams shut, leaving those who used to leave us feeling warm on the outside!

In an article about "leak-proof memory compartments," the author proposed a solution for better managing one's life by creating a multitude of tiny compartments that don't have any links between them. Therefore, the thoughts and emotions residing in each one wouldn't be contaminated by anything in adjoining compartments.

The way we relate to the one we once loved and now despise depends on the number of compartments flooded by their wrongdoings. If it exceeds a certain number, the contents will be irretrievably submerged into the dark abyss of our being, just like Titanic, which was tragically designed to only float with four flooded compartments, not five—which is what caused it to sink. So after that, no good memories will ever be able to rise to the surface.

I pray that you never have to deal with such a blow in respects to someone you once held fondly. Rather, I hope their memory can easily rise to the surface from the deep waters of your conscience, float calmly on the surface of the soul, and bathe in the warm rays of a nostalgic smile.

Kafka and the Doll

"Every day, Franz Kafka went for a walk in certain park, and one day, he encountered a little girl who was crying. She was devastated because she'd lost her doll and was inconsolable.

Kafka offered to help her look for the doll, but they couldn't find it. Comforted by his companionship, she asked him if he'd meet her the next day in the same spot, and he agreed. That night, he composed a letter from the doll, and read it to her when they met the next day.

'Please do not mourn me. I have gone on a trip to see the world. I will write you of my adventures. 'It was the first of many surprisingly upbeat letters. When he and the little girl met, he read her another episode in the imaginary adventures of the beloved doll. Again, the little girl was comforted.

When their meetings finally came to an end, Kafka presented her with a new doll. She obviously looked different from the original doll. An attached letter explained: 'My travels have changed me.'

After the girl had grown into a woman, she found a letter stuffed into an unnoticed crevice in the cherished replacement doll. It said, 'You'll eventually lose everything you love, but in the end, love will return in a different form...' "

Part III:

Building Healthy Relationships

Chapter 11: Childhood

"It's so easy to revert to a child's mind, but so hard to reach the heights of their souls!"
Romanian Expression

I'm the proud father of two daughters. And it just so happens that their participating chromosomes had won a beauty contest when they were both conceived, which explains why my offspring are so exquisite.

The physical resemblance between my two wonderful girls, Ruxandra and Georgia, is breathtaking! They look like twins who were born seven years apart. They say girls take after their fathers, but ever since they were little, they've looked like miniatures of my wife, except with my hair color.

When I praised Ruxandra for being clever, she replied: "Well, that's because I take after Mum!"

"And you bear no resemblance to Daddy?" I asked.

"Yes, I do: I have your ears!"

Then I asked her, as I did whenever I got the chance, "Tell me, dear, how beautiful are you?"

And she always answered with the word she uttered when she spoke for the first time as an infant: "Unspeakably!"

And I continued, "But how come you're so beautiful?"

"Because I've got good genes!"

"From whom, Ruxandra?"

"From Mummy *and* Daddy!"

Only on Odd Days

Ruxandra was about four years old when she stayed with my mother for an entire weekend for the first time. When my mother dropped her off, she told us about a memorable event.

Knowing her to be picky with her food, my mother concocted a strategy on her way to our house. Once they were alone, my mother approached her in a roundabout manner, saying, "Ruxandra, let's play host and guest. How about that? You'll be the host, and I'll be the guest. When the guest arrives, plates and flatware must be laid on the table, and then we'll eat: I take a bite, you take a bite, and so on..."

All the while, my daughter was paying attention to my mother, and she finally concluded with a mischievous smile: "You're so silly. I'm not going to eat anything anyway!"

Two years later, the two of them were again all by themselves for a few days. Of course, nothing had changed, and Ruxandra was still a picky eater. So coming back home, I asked (just to pass the time) how my daughter had eaten.

My mother replied: "I pled with her to eat, to no avail. At one point, I asked her, 'What are we going to tell your daddy?'

'We'll tell him I ate!' she said.

'Then, are we going to lie to daddy?'

After giving it a moment's thought, Ruxandra said, 'Yes, you're right, a lie is hard to get out of.'

I further insisted that she eat, until she exasperatedly ended the discussion and sharply said, 'Grandma, do please understand, I only eat on odd days!'

Needless to say, that entire conversation took place on an even day of Monday.

Richer at Heart

Then one evening, I was making dinner. Ruxandra said, "Daddy, I have a brilliant idea: What if I eat and watch cartoons at the same time? I take a bite and watch cartoons. I eat again and watch cartoons again!"

"Fine, Ruxandra, but be careful, or else you'll forget to take a bite while you're watching the cartoons, okay? And if that happens, I'll turn off the TV!"

"Yes, Daddy!"

I set up her little dining table in the living room, placed her little plate before her and left her with her cartoons.

Five minutes passed, and I returned to find that she hadn't touched her meal.

"Ruxandra, if you don't eat, I'll turn off the TV!"

"Yes, Daddy, I will eat!"

I left and returned after another five minutes: no change with the food, so I turned off the TV. All upset, she stood up and went to her room.

I could only stand this situation for two minutes before I checked on her. She was lying on her bed and staring at the ceiling. "What's going on, Ruxandra?"

"Well, I feel a little under the weather!" So I gave her some money to make her feel better, and she her reaction was, "Wow, I'm rich!"

I explained that it is more important to have a rich heart than deep pockets. Without hesitation, she replied, "I understand: You gave me some money, and now I'm richer at heart because I can buy chocolate!"

Future Attorney?

Ruxandra has incredible debate skills – and of course, she did not inherit this quality from me...

One Saturday, we scheduled an outing to the mall, and I said to her, "Practice your piano, or I won't take you with me."

"Daddy, please, take me with you. I promise I'll play when we get back!"

"No, Ruxandra, no way. You know very well that you can only reap what you sow. No one can reap before they sow!"

"Tit for tat!" she replied.

"Exactly, that's right!" I exclaimed.

"Ah no, that's for you, Daddy. If you do good and take me to the mall, then you'll get your reward: I'll play the piano!"

Here's another story that confirms her persuasive skills. We had a small argument at home. I showed my authority by asking her to do something that did not sit well with her. She rudely responded, "I don't want to. You're not the boss in this house!"

"You reckon you're the boss?!" I replied.

"Yes, I am!"

"Reason that out for me."

After a moment, she found her reasoning: "I am the boss because we have a pretty house that needs a pretty boss like me!"

More recently, Ruxandra has established some "house rules" for my wife and me as a couple. Here's the last one: "Love each other like two nightingales meeting for the first time, gazing into each other's eyes and forming an unforgettable couple!" How could we forget such a rule?

Thoughts on Talent

One evening, Ruxandra was preparing her schoolbag for her next day in first grade, and I saw her sneaking a small note to herself into her pencil case that said: Love, Talent, Cleverness.

I asked her what the note was referring to. "Well, today, the teacher read us a parable and assigned us homework to think of three character traits that Good God has bestowed on us. And I thought of these three. Actually, wait a minute!" She erased the word "talent" and replaced it with "mercy." "Because it's more important to be merciful than talented."

At Christmastime, Ruxandra was assigned the role of the Mother of Christ in the 1st grade school play, and she was rehearsing the lyrics. At one point, she was being silly—as children often are—reciting them in a monotonous style while staring at the floor. "Ruxandra, stop staring at the floor!" Gina admonished her.

Her instant reply was, "The Mother of Christ may gaze at whatever she wishes!"

On the first of March, I called my mother to give her my monthly well-wishes. Ruxandra announced, "Grandma, I have a musical March wish for you!" I put the phone on speaker, and she played a song on the piano.

Afterward, my mother said: "Ruxandra, I have a March wish for you: Do know that you are the most loved granddaughter in the whole world?"

And she replied: "My, oh my, I'm going to faint!"

A Beakless Bird

"Daddy, you know my soul is sensitive like that of a beakless bird!"

That's what Ruxandra told me as she was crying during one of our disputes, which ended with temporary revoked "privileges of the under aged" (such as access to the android and iPad).

"What do you mean?" I asked.

"Well, a beakless bird is very sad, since it cannot sing anymore!" This explanation once again left me speechless. (We have a really special little girl.)

I don't know how Georgia will turn out, as she is only a toddler. But Ruxandra has a truly sensitive soul, which I deem to be an extraordinary quality! Of course, it does have its shortfalls, but it must not be mistaken for weakness. A sensitive person holds a superior capacity for perceiving their surroundings and the complexities of their personalities will be the measuring sticks. The expression of their feelings will be rich, and people flooded with feelings will feel their blessings to the fullest. A lack of reciprocity from those around them will probably cause pain, perhaps to a greater extent than someone whose sensitivity has a higher threshold. But the benefits are incomparable. That's why we do all we can to delicately nurture the souls of our daughters.

The Little Heart

I found the parable below in Andrei Patranca's blog. He is a former student of mine, who's now a renowned psychiatrist. It's one of the most emotional parables I've ever read.

"One day, a small heart looked into the mirror and examined herself carefully. And when she saw her reflection, she stood in amazement and joy at how she beat rhythmically (filling each corner of her chambers with the fluid of life), how she kept so little for herself, and how she sent everything else out into the universe! But what surprised her most was seeing how every piece of news, be it good or bad, affected her beating, and made her laugh heartily or cry tears of blood.

Once, she received a big volume of demand from the muscles and the brain. She strived with all her might to deliver even more blood, but she didn't succeed. She cried out to a larger heart and asked for a strong hug, to pump out more to the organs that had asked for her help. But instead of a hug, she received a hard slap on the face. Then the little heart saddened and cried a lot. And from then on, a feeling of uncertainty, of strain, of fear that it "wouldn't be capable" was discretely instilled in her.

One day, she approached several hearts that were laughing, playing and dancing. 'May I join you?' she asked them, full of hope.

'Don't mess with our playtime!' The other hearts turned their back on her and kept playing. From then on, sadness and misery entered the little heart, so she cried a lot.

One day, the little heart took her backpack and joyfully ran off to school. The teacher gave them a hard test, and it didn't go well. So when the heart went home, she cried: 'Mum, mum, look what happened to me!' The mother's heart turned black with fury and started screaming: 'What grade did Jane get? Ah, higher than you? I told you that you were a good-for-nothing. I wish you were never born. You're just like your father!'

These words deeply wounded the little heart. And from then on, she developed a feeling that she had no value and was inherently flawed.

From that moment on, the little heart chose to hide herself behind a cold mask of chest bones. She stopped asking for help or trying to live with all her being. When there was something to laugh about, she no longer laughed, and when there was something to cry about, she no longer cried. And she no longer had the courage to look at herself in the mirror or let others discover her the way she was.

She learned how to smile without feeling and sigh without showing it. Hurt and tried all over, she hoped, deep inside, that there would come a day when all the other hearts would give her the hug she longed for so much, that they would let her play with them and cherish her the way she was.

This could be the story of your heart and my heart, as well."

For some people, life is an iconic tear traveling down the cheek to the soul...

We're All Born Prince Charming

When we are young, we don't have the capacity to foresee danger or distinguish right from wrong. So we frequently subject our souls to the cold blaze of the wind and express ourselves with the candor that is so specific to youth.

Only two fears are stored in our genetic makeup at birth: the fear of noise and the fear of falling. In all other matters, we are born fearless, like Prince Charming. That's why we charge on, full of confidence, into the whirlpool of life. And yes, we will invariably burn ourselves from time to time, until our soul is well-done and is permeated by the unpleasant odors of experience. Our self-confidence can even be burned to ashes. But thankfully, God gave us the resilience to be reborn like a phoenix rising from the ashes!

Likewise, studies have shown that, until they're three years old, all children have the conviction that they're good people—if their parents love them and encourage them to explore their surroundings. (Perhaps that's also why the moment of truth in relationships occurs at the three-year point. People are literally trained from birth to give everyone the benefit of the doubt for three years!)

Conversely, even two-year-olds can believe that there's something wrong with them if they're unceasingly criticized. Even if they can't put their finger on it, they instinctively assume that their parents know the truth, and that they deserve the suffering that eats them up inside.

Unfortunately, the deepest wounds are produced by those closest to our soul. Especially when we're children, the blows we receive from our parents extend much deeper into the pits of our souls because we don't have the armor to withstand such aggression. It seems unlikely that those meant to protect us—who have been entrusted with our souls—are the very ones that would hit it so hard that the resulting wounds would cause permanent scars that can be reactivated and ache from time to time.

These blows can result in chronic conditions that will accompany us throughout our lives as emotional gangrene that invariably results in the amputation of the soul since there is no prosthesis for such a thing. Therefore, we, the adults, are bestowed with the extraordinarily delicate and difficult mission of safeguarding the hearts of our children, so they won't be scarred for life.

The Childhood Fir

One day, I was coming back with Ruxandra from an event where her class had adorned a tree, and she told me they called it "the childhood fir." And she was somewhat dissatisfied, because in her opinion, it was not a childish tree. I told her: "Ruxandra, if it's a childhood tree, it doesn't necessarily mean it's childish. They only call it that to remind you it was part of your childhood later on!"

She pondered this thought for a while, then said: "Remembering your childhood is the most beautiful gift."

I looked at her, a little surprised: "Where did you hear that?"

"Nowhere, Daddy. It just came to me."

No matter how our lives were as children, it's never too late to have a happy childhood. But the second one is all up to us...

The Kisses from the Box

"The story goes that one day a man punished his 5-year-old girl because she squandered every expensive piece of gold wrapping paper.

The man was having some financial problems and became angry when he saw that the little girl had used the paper to decorate a box and put it under the Christmas tree.

However, the next morning, the little girl brought her father the gift. 'This is for you, daddy!'

He felt ashamed about his angry reaction, but his annoyance returned when he saw that the box was actually empty. 'Little lady, you didn't know that when you offer someone a gift, you have to put something inside it?'

Tears welled up in the little girl's eyes, and she said: 'But the box isn't empty, daddy! I kept blowing kisses into it until I filled it up.'

The father was dumbfounded. He kneeled down, hugged the little girl, and asked her to forgive him for his unkindness.

Since that day, the man has kept that golden box next to his bed. And whenever he felt discouraged or went through a difficult situation, he opened the box, took an imaginary kiss, and remembered all the love the little girl put in there.

Each of us receives a golden box with unconditional love and kisses from our children. We cannot have anything more precious than that. But do we know how to appreciate what we get?"

Chapter 12: Friendship

"A true friend is always on time, but a fair-weather friend only helps you when he has time."
Romanian Expression

"Once upon a time, long ago, there was a rose that thought itself to be the most beautiful flower in the field. It would often brag, 'There's no other more beautiful than me!'

One cool morning, a dandelion blossomed right next to the rose.

'Would you be friends with me?' the dandelion asked.

'Me?! I don't need a friend! Beauty is my only friend!' the rose answered.

After a while, a little girl came to pick a flower for her mother. She wanted to pick the rose. But the dandelion ordered the wind to blow softly, so it would flutter. Then the little girl changed her mind and plucked the dandelion instead of the rose. Its eyes wet with tears, the rose looked at the dandelion that had sacrificed itself to save the rose. Since then, the rose has never stopped searching for a devoted friend."

Tears came to my eyes when I read this short story, written by Ruxandra! My wonderful little girl astonished me once again with the depth of her thought, and most of all, her feelings. How did she manage, with her child's mind and soul, to express in such an emotional manner the impact that some human traits have upon us—from the arrogance of the rose to the sublime generosity and sacrifice of the dandelion?

Gandhi once said that friendship is like a diamond: it's rare, it's worth a lot and it's often falsified. A true friend cannot be found at the end of the road. He is there, by your side. You walk together on the road of life, and he remains beside you, regardless of how steep the path might become or of the chasms that open from place to place. A true friend knows your flaws, values your good traits and acknowledges your limits while trusting your capabilities. He feels your doubts but strengthens your faith. He can see the rose petals and doesn't get hurt by its thorns. He is a part of you mirrored in himself. He is priceless. He understands what you once were and accepts what you have become.

He looks you in the eye and says, "I cannot give you answers to all of life's problems, and I don't have a solution for each of your fears. But I can patiently listen to you and understand you and take part in your struggle. I cannot remove obstacles that you trip over along your path, but I can lend you a hand if you fall and help you get back on your feet. I cannot help ease your suffering when pain tears your soul apart, but I can weep with you and comfort you by picking up the fallen pieces of your soul in my hand, until you enjoy life and have gratitude in your heart."

Therefore, let us have the wisdom to surround ourselves with people who:
- Make us happy.
- Help us when we're in need.

- Never take advantage of us because they care about us.

They are as rare as precious jewels that deserve to be kept in our lives at any cost since all others are just passing by. And the best friend is the one that stays!

Rose-Colored Friendship

"A wise man's apprentice made a huge mistake, and everybody was expecting the master to punish him. But the master behaved as if nothing had happened. After a month, another apprentice came to him and resentfully said, 'Master, I cannot believe that you didn't say anything to him when you saw what a mistake he'd made! That's why God gave us mouths!'

Smiling, the wise man answered, 'But He also gave us eyelids.' "

Unless we turn a blind eye to the small mistakes of our friends, we will not be able to enjoy their great qualities.

Pick Your Battles

It's a great thing to know when to let things slide, too. The instinctual reaction of our "ego" is to defend its wealth, be it material or spiritual wealth. It's very interesting how most of the times we lead the hardest battle to protect our spiritual assets, our beliefs on which the entire scaffolding of our being is founded, although their use value is extremely relative – what we deem to be authentic and valuable, others will perceive as lacking consistency. And this is where numerous conflictual situations arise throughout a day by interacting with varied people who merely see the world in different colors.

In the end, this is not an issue in itself. It occurs because they also see our world differently, reducing its dimensions and invalidating our beliefs. Although, I don't know who will gladly bear the trammels (except for masochists). Even Vivian Leigh, who ardently wished to attract the attention of wooers, made grimaces at Mammy while the latter was putting on her corset on her frail body in *Gone with the Wind*.

So, I see it as a proof of great wisdom to concede before someone who is attempting to vehemently impose their beliefs. They say that if you are wrong, you get reprimanded and keep quiet, so you are wise. And if you are right, you get reprimanded and keep quiet, so you are married.

Diving in with all arguments in a dispute will always end in failure. Because if your partner comes with a series of irrefutable counterarguments, you will lose; if your argument goes in your favor, you will lose again – the wounded pride of the defeated will remember it.

Of course, the approach that I recommend refers to minor disputes that might emerge one day, but will have no permanent impact. It goes without saying that we should defend some moral principles that have direct or long-term consequences.

Accounting for Life

The longevity of life should not be calculated by adding up the days that have passed, rather those that you remember because of someone or something.

That thought flashed through me one evening as I was returning with Ruxandra from piano lessons. I felt its striking truth not as the flickering flicker of a candle, but as the dazzling headlights of cars in the night. It hit me: I didn't know how much of my life had gone by – as if I hadn't lived for long periods of time. I can imagine what a terrible disease Alzheimer's can be – to only live today's moments and a few fragments of the past.

How precious memories can be if we know how to attach value to them! What I mean by value is wrapping them up beautifully in a specially designed box in our brain and opening it throughout our life to feed our soul by reliving emotions we once experienced. For example, when Ruxandra was two years old, I had the idea to create a file intended for the memorable moments to come with having children. So I started to record the "pearls" she uttered with her wonderful little mouth (I have already shared some of them with you), and each day I would open the file to write down another memorable "punch line", which automatically also became an occasion to relive past emotions.

Happy are those who have decided to enjoy at least one such present every day! Happy are those who dearly dive in the ocean of their memories, those who know how to treasure those special moments that have enchanted them throughout their lives! Happy are those who keep in their affective memory all those who have made them feel alive, whether they are still in their lives or not. As long as they have put a mark on our existence, one way or the other, for one day or for a thousand days or if their actions have been instilled in our DNA's purine and pyrimidine bases, they must be cherished, even if only at a memory level. *What life has separated, memories can reunite.*

The price of a child`s joy

The musing on accounting the days of our lives was fresh in my mind the moment I decided to get involved in a campaign for likes on Facebook. Ruxandra's class was competing against other 12 classes in some schools in Sibiu – they each adorned a Christmas tree at a spa centre in the city, and the class that would accumulate the highest number of likes was to be declared as the winner. With 320 likes, her class was in second place a week before the end of voting with a difference of 100 likes compared to the class in first place.

And so, I started to engage my friends, colleagues, students, parents, brothers, uncles, cousins and aunts, and the competition turned out to be extremely exciting as the voting went on. If in the first two weeks there was a large gap between the classes in the first two spots, I had the satisfaction of knowing that in two days, we moved into the first place in a short time, which further fueled the competition. Each evening they were ahead of us by 100 – 150 votes, and in the day before the end of the competition, they were ahead by 300 votes.

On the last day, when I picked up Ruxandra from her after-school lessons, we had to recover a gap of 500 votes in six hours! Knowing how hard it had been to collect all the likes in previous days, I started to prepare her for defeat. I explained the "state of things" to her, telling her that we can't win all the time and that failure is a part of life. We would do better next time!

I admit, I had lost almost all hope; it would have taken a miracle to change the fate of the voting. And the miracle did happen! We started to gradually recover the gap, and at one point, things happened so fast that we barely realized we'd won when we beat them! Incredibly, in six mere hours we'd made up for the 500-vote deficit – and added another 500 votes to that, resulting in a first place finish. Ruxandra's joy was immeasurable!

Not long after the competition closed, I posted the following message on Facebook: "Friends, the other day, when I asked you to help me with the Christmas tree campaign, I mentioned that the joy in your child's eyes is priceless. Ten minutes ago, when I told Ruxandra that we won, I saw you – all those who cared about me and my little girl – in her bright eyes. So that you know: you have also become priceless for me."

This experience again showed me how much it matters to care about those around you! There were friends whose involvement was completely lacking, and there were friends who competed against themselves to help me. Why? Because they cared, because they knew they could not change the world, but they could change the world of one person – the world of my little girl.

As adults, we regularly fight battles that are far more important than a trivial Christmas tree competition, but for her and her colleagues this was the challenge of the moment. And some of those I resorted to understood this. Throughout life, we do not meet too many people who care enough to get involved or committed to something. When we do meet them, it's best to keep them close.

The Constellations of Our Lives

When we seek advice or need space to vent, we should truly appreciate our friends' availability. Ultimately, they have the option of refusing to get involved and opting for options with more positive outcomes for them. Of course, these are the moments that reveal our true friends. These friends can be compared to constellations: We don't always see them, but we feel them shining in our hearts every time we go through hard times.

The most beautiful gift you can give someone is your time because you are giving a slice of your life that you will never get back! I think this world would be a better place if people were aware of this truth, if for no reason than your disposition will change if you receive presents every day. Time isn't just any type of present; it's the equivalent of the complete surrender of a part of someone's life.

Therefore, I long ago reached the conclusion that time is an extremely valuable currency. That's why time can be invested or spent, just as money can.

I'll admit that I wasted a lot of time until I fully recognized its value. I wasted time in front of the TV, on the phone, in bed, participating in useless chit-chat.

However, the time we grant to a friend in need represents one of the best investments we can make in life. It validates us as human beings. It proves we care, which is extremely valuable. It strengthens our reputation and the respect we receive from others. Once we've helped a friend get out of a of a trench they might find themselves in, we can see them looking to us with gratitude as they say: "I don't know where my life is headed, dear friend, but my path is better when I'm holding your hand!"

So think twice before you say no to a friend who asks you for help. You might be the only one able to help him…

Dog's Best Friend

"A man named Saul and a dog were walking on a road. Saul was enjoying the beautiful day when he suddenly remembered that the dog walking by his side had long left the world of the living years before.

Then Saul realized he'd also died. But he was bizarrely calm and asked himself: 'Where does this road lead?'

After a while, they reached a tall stone wall. Looking at it closely, Saul could see that it was made of very fine marble. Up the hill, the wall ended at a gate that was shining in the sun. When they got there, he could see it had a pearl inlay, and the road leading to it was paved in gold. He and the dog approached the gate, and he saw an old man sitting at a table to the side of it. He asked the man: 'Pardon me, where are we?'

'This is heaven,' the old man answered.

'Wonderful! Could you please give us some water?' Saul asked.

'Of course, come in.' The old man made a gesture, and the gate opened.

'Can my friend come, too?' Saul asked, pointing at the dog.

'I'm sorry, but we don't allow animals inside.'

Saul pondered for a second, then turned and continue down the road with his dog.

After climbing a tall hill, they arrived at the gate of a farm, which seemed like it had never had a fence, much less a marble wall! Examining it more closely, he saw a man leaning on a tree and reading a book.

'Excuse me!' Saul said as he approached him.

'Do you happen to have some water?'

'But of course. There's a water pump right over there.'

'Can my friend use it, too?' he said, pointing at the dog.

'There must be a bowl nearby.'

They passed the gate and reached an old water pump. Saul and the dog quenched their thirst. When they finished, they went back to the man under the tree.

'What place is this?' Saul asked.

'This is heaven!'

'I'm totally confused. Someone down the road told me that he lived in heaven.'

'You mean that place with the marble walls and glimmering vault? That's hell.'

'And you don't mind they're using the same name as you do?'

'On the contrary, we're glad they screen the ones that are ready to leave their best friends behind...' "

Chapter 13: Romance

"She sings, and I listen. On her warm lips, my soul is born."
Lucian Blaga

This Romanian poet and philosopher provided a brilliant definition of a *coup de foudre*.

Over the centuries, love has reached the hearts of innumerable creatives, many of whom possess an extraordinary amount of sensitivity. They made these wonderful observations about the changes that occur under love's spell:

- "When we leave each other's sides, we don't feel like we're breaking apart, but going to wait for each other in another place."
- "Why do you love him? You won't be together anyway! Why do you breathe? You'll die anyway!"
- "In your absence, I am the only piece missing inside me. You are always there!"
- "I must be out of my mind, but I hope I'm in yours."
- "You took me in your arms, and I took you in my soul. But while arms can get tired, the soul never does!"
- "When you're in love, you're alive! The rest of the time, you just exist…"
- And my favorite one: "When love can no longer fit in two hearts, a third one is born."

Are you experiencing the type of infatuation Blaga described? If so, you're probably wondering if it will turn out to be true love. Maybe it will, maybe it won't. For right now, we're just going to examine the butterflies in the stomach that are hatched from the larvae of love—the frenzied flutter to the balcony, where we can catch a glimpse of our newfound infatuation!

That Loving Feeling

There are some very scientific reasons why we feel the way we do at the beginning of a romance. For instance, let's take a look at why lovers close their eyes when they kiss. As emotions run high and excitement overtakes their entire being, the body reacts by discharging adrenaline, which speeds up the heartbeat, pumps out more blood and prepares the muscles for potential activity... In addition, adrenaline produces mydriasis (dilation of the pupils), so that a large amount of light will reach the retinas. The reflex reaction to this effect is closing the eyes.

This phenomenon seems to be sensibly tempered in men by a characteristic that's statistically proven to be more likely in men than women: We tend to be visually stimulated. So dear female readers, if you happen to open your eyes during a passionate kiss and see your lover intently gazing at you with his eyes wide open, don't accuse him of being detached. He's just enjoying the view!

The Fast Pass to the Inner Chamber

While external beauty may open doors, inner beauty opens the gates to souls, and behind those gates lie the true riches that one should seek in life. Let's find out what frequently happens!

The appearance of a beautiful person in our visual range creates a stimulation of the rod-and-cone cells in our retinas that makes us want to look at them. It's an instinctive reaction that is related to our individual preferences as they relate to physical appearance.

Apparently, God has given the people we find beautiful a gift, which is similar to a fast pass (you know, that ticket that allows you quicker access to tourist attractions). It streamlines their path to the front door of your inner chamber.

But once they get there, they'll benefit from exactly the same rights as those that bought a regular ticket. In other words, just because they got into the room faster doesn't mean they'll win your heart once they get there. In order to make a connection last, there has to be soul-to-soul dialogue, not a just a soul-to-outer-beauty dialogue.

You probably already know that beauty is only skin deep, but ugliness can extend all the way to the bone. Remember, a wolf in sheep's clothing is still a wolf!

Butterflies or Bad Burrito?

The scientific reasons for puppy love don't stop with the eyes.

I can also make an efficient, differential diagnosis between the digestive manifestations of love (e.g., the previously mentioned butterflies) and other physiological symptoms in the body, such as a gastric pathology. This differentiation is all the more important for young people who are inexperienced in the field of love.

When in doubt, an upper gastrointestinal (GI) endoscopy procedure can be performed that shows whether the butterflies that a person feels are, in fact, produced by gastritis!

Definitions

The great medical professor Iuliu Hatieganu said that love is the most serious disease of all, since it makes two individuals bedridden at the same time!

It has been proven that young lovers often suffer from insomnia, and its idiopathic nature is yet another cause for debate among researchers. Some claim that a comfortable bed and two individuals in love cannot lead to drowsiness. Others say this insomnia is due to the fact that they realize that what is happening to them is more beautiful than any dream…

Heartbeats for headaches – that would be one of the definitions for love. Honestly, I don't know anyone who has ever taken any painkillers for that kind of migraine. Another definition is "a feeling that comes in galloping and leaves on tiptoe." I don't know if it bears any connection to that galloping sound you hear in a stethoscope when examining someone with a heart disease. But I do know that when I met my future wife, I felt like a team of horses were suddenly trotting into my soul. Fortunately, they're still there, frantically neighing every day.

In medical school, I also learned the clinical manifestation of the sweet retrosternal burden that each and every lover has felt so many times: dyspnea or shortness of breath. And of course, there are related manifestations: the previously mentioned mydriasis, shivers and tremors, tachypnea (abnormally rapid breathing) and, yes, scorching breath. Shakespeare said that love is the mist born in the steam of sighs. So the next time a dense mist envelops the car you're driving, don't let it put you in a bad mood; it's simply because there are so many lovers around!

Love is an Hourglass

When the heart fills up, the brain empties out.

In this ingenious definition of love, we find the answer to a question that frequently arises in the minds of those who have loved, then have suddenly awoken from its spell: "What was I thinking?" Well, you all have just found out the answer: "Nothing!"

Love has the unique capability of completely liquefying the brain's grey matter, until it entirely leaks into the left atrium of the heart. And from there, it passes into the left ventricle and forcefully pumps all over our entire being.

And when a heart is filled up…well, you know the sensation, don't you? It causes:
- Waves of warmth we would bathe in incessantly.
- Wings that grow out of us like a Pegasus.
- An unquenchable thirst for life.

143

- An impatient longing to be in the presence of our significant other, and the elongation of time in their absence.

No sober or lucid analysis matters; only the merged experience of the two parties has meaning.

We all know what a remarkable organ the brain is. It operates nonstop, 24 hours a day, 7 days a week, 365 days a year—from birth until the day you fall in love! Fortunately, the brain can regenerate very easily. In fact, Ruxandra made this comment a few seconds after hearing the comparison of love to an hourglass: "Aha! And after a while, you turn the hourglass upside down, right?"

Love and Genetic Engineering

We get to the boiling point at different temperatures. Even lovers show this discrepancy. But that's irrelevant as long as they're both well-done!

We all have flaws. Some of them overlap in people who are in love with each other, so it's easy to turn a blind eye to them. After a while, other flaws are perceived as antigens that may catalyze a full-out rejection of the other person, similar to the body's reaction to a skin graft.

In such cases, there are two solutions:
- "Immunosuppressive treatment", which requires self-medication by therapeutically accepting our partner's flaws. In other words, if you want your relationship to last, deal with the flaws, and keep your mouth shut!
- "Genetic engineering", which aims to alter the antigen structure that bothers us. Well, that's where the trouble starts, since we insist on

asking for a change from someone who has likely reached an age when he or she claims to be mature enough to decide on the set of values that he or she will adhere to.

As the classic Romanian song goes:

> You know people don't change.
> Why did you want to change me?
> To look at me like in a mirror?'

Keep in mind that the climax of this phase of a relationship occurs after about three years. Before reaching that stage, we have to deal with the way our heart reasons with us, which is completely different than the way the brain does. As they say: *In any romantic relationship, there's a Romeo, a Juliet, and a balcony, where you'll eventually air out your laundry!*

Love Is Blindness

"Love at first sight...Why does it happen so often? Because people do not realize that the person they've fallen in love with has a plethora of flaws: greed, malice, stubbornness." That's what Ruxandra wrote on my laptop, during a five-minute break from being an eight-year-old. And she's right.

No one is saying that you shouldn't follow your heart. But you'd better take your brain with you because its software is capable of identifying viruses that have infected your value system regarding the person your heart is on fire for. However, I'll admit: This goal isn't easy to achieve!

As the brain melts at the intensity of the soul's burning flames, its clarity of vision in identifying character alterations is close to null. That's why they say love is blind. So let's at least allow ourselves to be caressed!

Spinning this concept in a different way, let's relate eyesight to lasciviousness: many men's thoughts are inversely proportional to how low-cut a woman's blouse is. When these men see cleavage, their brains start madly groping around and losing soberness of thought, sometimes even the power of speech.

I call this phenomenon the "ocular-cerebral mammary reflex." You won't find this reflex in any neurophysiology treatises since the studies I've conducted only comprise of a few dozen male friends of mine. In other words, my research isn't extensive enough. But the percentage of my interviewees who confirmed the existence of this reflex was 100%!

So what exactly is the ocular-cerebral mammary reflex? The moment a woman appears on the horizon, these men's eyes send information to their brain, which immediately commands them to focus on her breasts. I don't believe this reflex is connected to the memory of breasts that fed us when we were young: all men weren't breast-fed, and this reflex isn't present in people who aren't attracted to women, regardless if they breastfed as babies![8]

In these men, the sight of a more or less revealed breast leads to a magically melting of ligaments that keep eye bulbs in their sockets, which

---

[8]This reflex is not present in most physicians, since good doctors look at women with a clinician's eye, void of any trace of testosterone.

results in their eyes rolling down into the cleavage that appeared on the horizon. Left in pitch-black, the brain loses its skill of judgement, and its owner will abruptly have his IQ significantly diminished. That's why, dear female readers, it's vital that the intelligence level of a potential male partner should be assessed when you're wearing a turtleneck and a heavy coat.

Love is a Battlefield

"Before heading to battle, an American soldier went into the National Library in New York, where his attention was drawn by a book of poetry. It wasn't the poems themselves, although some of them were truly beautiful. Rather, it was the comments that the book's original owner had written next to some of them. The soldier took the book with him on the battlefield, and because the woman had recorded her name and address on the inside cover, he sent her a letter, in which he confessed how impressed he was with her comments.

To his surprise, he received a letter in reply. They started a correspondence, getting to know each other more and more. Gradually, strong feelings grew between them.

Eventually, the soldier asked her, 'Please send me a picture of you. I really wish I could see what you look like!' Her prompt answer was: 'My dear, if your feelings are as strong as I can feel they are in the letters you've sent me, my appearance really shouldn't matter!'

Even though she never sent him her picture, they kept corresponding. When the war was over, they decided to meet in Grand Central Station. They agreed on these ways to recognize each other: He would hold her book of poetry in his hand, and she would hold a rose.

And so on a beautiful afternoon in the month of May, a soldier getting back from the battlefield anxiously waited to meet the love of his life!

His attention was immediately drawn by a gorgeous young woman wearing a green suit who was intensely looking at him, but his heart almost stopped when he saw that the woman had nothing in her hand.

Standing a few feet behind her was a much less attractive woman holding the much-awaited rose! As he crossed the station, the soldier could feel himself getting flustered. When he reached the woman in green, she asked him directly: 'Hi soldier, are you going my way?' He hesitated for a few seconds, and she disappeared into the crowd.

The feelings ruling his soul belonged to the woman holding the rose. Deeply moved, he declared, 'Oh, how glad I am to finally meet you!'

The second woman replied, 'Soldier, I don't know what's going on here, but that girl in the green suit asked me to hold this rose and tell you, if you come to me, that she's waiting for you in the restaurant on the corner.' "

So she was eloquent, beautiful, and wise – a killer combination!

Keep this story in mind when considering the "solutions" that genetic engineering is offering, which will allow us to filter out "imperfections." These developments could create problems in a world that's already obsessed with appearance. As a result, these kinds of statements could soon have a different meaning: "If you love someone, you love them the way they are, not the way you want them to be!"

Chapter 14: Marriage

"The difficulty in a marriage derives from the fact that we fall for a person, but we have to live with their personality."
Peter De Vries

I will never forget the image of my Grandmother Sylvia lying still in her coffin, her arms crossed over her chest. She was holding two wedding bouquets—both bunches of dried field basil—in her hands. She kept them for 68 and 74 years, respectively. One was from her first husband, who died in World War II, and the second was from her second husband Alion, my grandfather. It was her dying wish to be buried with both of them.

She was that committed to the institution of marriage!

More Bile than Honey

Love blossoms with a smile, grows with a kiss and ends with tears. "Why does that happen?" a friend asked me once. "Why do feelings and emotions fade over time? Why do marriages grow stale?"

"Each couple has its own unique experience," I replied. "Maybe that's how things are meant to be: With love, you kill time. But with time, you kill love."

During a marriage, there is a time for love and a time for toil. For whatever reason, it seems mandatory that love occurs before toil, and not vice versa. As the old Latin said: *Qui amat, non laboriat*! So after about three years, you sober up. Bit by bit, you start tasting something other than honey.

As time goes by, if you end up offering more bile than honey, there will be trouble in paradise. That's why it's very important to have your eyes wide open before getting married and to keep them half-closed after the wedding day. Many times, the difference between successful and failed marriages is ignoring the two or three little things that annoyed you about your partner throughout the day.

The Only Thing I Regret about Paris

Referring back to the concept of a honeymoon, many people think of it as more of a trip than a time period. Likewise, one way to reignite the passion in a marriage is to take your spouse on a romantic trip to celebrate your anniversary.

In May 2010, I went to a travel agency to prepare my vacation. We wanted to go to an island in Greece or Turkey. Eventually, the agent told me that another one of her customers had given a cruise of the Mediterranean to her husband as a surprise on their anniversary. Suddenly, an idea dawned in my frontal lobe: What if I make a similar surprise to my wife on our ten-year wedding anniversary in September? Said and done!

First, I'd have to set the location: I'd never heard of any other place more romantic than Paris! So I made reservations for plane tickets and a hotel room, maintaining the utmost secrecy.

At the beginning of September, Gina and I were watching the TV show *The Bachelor*, which was

151

taking place in Paris. Watching the footage performed on various locations in the City of Lights, I heard her sighing: "How great would it be if we were in Paris on our marriage anniversary!"I concealed my smile of joy and vowed not to reveal my secret since I didn't want to ruin the surprise!

On September 18, we celebrated our ten years of marriage at the Ramada hotel with forty family members and friends. At the start of the party, I took the microphone and thanked all of them for being with us on that occasion. However, I didn't thank them all together as a group. No, I made each friend stand up, and I emphasized some of the qualities I appreciated about them in a few sentences. I even thanked Lucica, the leader of the band that sang and delighted us that evening. He was the first man to have ever brought tears to my eyes when he sang to me the day after Ruxandra was born, at about four o'clock in the morning.

Finally, I asked, "Have I forgotten anyone?" As if on cue, they answered in unison: "Gina!" Of course I had a little speech ready for her, too, and at the end, I added: "I guess, my dear, you are expecting an anniversary present as well. Well, in the spirit of what happened ten years ago, here is my present for you!" (On our wedding night, she made a romantic reservation for us at the Nuptial Suite at the Romans' Emperor Hotel, where the ceremony was held, while I pragmatically gave her a cellphone.)

I made a discrete sign, and a waiter appeared carrying a suitcase. "What's inside?" she asked.

"Another suitcase," I said.

"And in the second suitcase?"

"Nothing. What else would be in there? But if you want something romantic, please dance with me!"

I made another discrete sign to the DJ, and the song "Ten" by Florin Chilian started pouring out of the speakers.

My wife's first reaction while we were dancing (which I could have predicted would happen), was "What about this present?"

Then I gave the final signal, and slides appeared on the two plasma screens near the dancefloor. They were fake photos of Gina and me in various locations in Paris: The Eiffel Tower, The Notre Dame Cathedral, Versailles and Moulin Rouge. Each of them were dated between September 20 - 25, 2010. Then she realized where we were going!

The trip became one of the best memories of our lives. After we went to Versailles, we had lunch nearby, and I told her, "Dear, put something classy on tonight. I want to take pictures of us in front of Moulin Rouge, after we go to the show there!"

One of my wife's qualities is her ability to keep calm in stressful situations, but at that moment, she was overwhelmed with emotions. She was actually shaking!

Why such a reaction? Well, Gina has been blessed with acting skills that could have secured her a career onstage. In fact, she holds many prizes in different competitions and festivals, including one handed over by Adrian Paunescu! So when preparing the surprise, I told myself that a live show at the famous Moulin Rouge wasn't something to be missed. I had bought tickets for the first show of the day. While it included dinner, it's not the reason why

I chose it. I'd read on internet that the orchestra would give a signal at a certain point before the show, and all attendees could go onstage and dance! To give my wife that kind of opportunity—as much as she loves all things theatre and cabaret—would be the cherry on top!

And yes, I savored it in full, dear readers. At one point, the orchestra started playing a waltz, and out of all the people on stage, we were the only ones who knew how to waltz! So we got applause while we were on stage at Moulin Rouge.

The only thing I regret about the Paris trip is that I don't know how I'll ever be able to top it.

Marital Memory Banks

There are two theories about how to argue with your wife. Unfortunately, neither one of them works...

It's been scientifically proven that more women than men have extraordinary memories that allow them to drag out the past with an extraordinary efficiency! So, men are less likely to win arguments, and the explanation is very simple: The hippocampus plays a decisive role in storing information, and it's overwhelmed with receptors for estrogen. When testosterone reaches the hippocampus, it stands and looks at it bewildered like a calf before a new gate (a Romanian saying), behind which memories hardly push through. The estrogen-caressed receptor allows the hippocampus to operate like a buzzer that opens the gate whenever necessary.

In many marriages, husbands easily forget their mistakes. After all, there's no point in both people remembering the same thing...

Do you remember the scene in *Bruce Almighty* when Jim Carrey's character wants to review the file about his life, but the instant he pulls the drawer out, it expands by about 20 meters? Well, many wives have thousands of these files that comprise a seemingly infinite amount of information, including files on their husbands' personal life, social life and professional life.

In their turn, these files can have well-defined subclasses, such as:

- "Days when he made a mistake"
- "His indolence"
- "Hours when I was suffering in silence, and he was out with the guys"
- "Weekends full of football, not me"
- "The 16 times he didn't notice I changed my hairstyle"

As an agent from the CIA, Mossad and KGB would tell you: "Information rules a situation!" Women won't say it, but many they wield information with incredible skill. All the more, their intuition—which allows them to contradict their spouses before they even open their mouths—invariably enhances the incredible memory they were already blessed with.

And when a wife's peroration brutally crushes against the

Hard wll of her husband's bewilderment discountenance, and annoyance (since behind an upset woman there is often a man who has no idea what he did wrong), she may resort to one of the most effective weapons in the history of mankind: tears. But we know a woman's tears are more dangerous than hydrofluoric acid!

And if we were to believe the Talmud, which says that God counts a woman's tears, what are the chances a man can win a dispute with a woman? (Especially if he's married to an attorney, like I am!)

The Ripple Effect

But as they say, every blessing has a curse. Perhaps overactive memories cause some women to prioritize incorrectly.

Years ago, I noticed that *on the road of life, men only trip over rocks, but women can trip over dust!* For many husbands, it is bewildering and impossible to understand how many issues can emerge from nothing. An apparently innocent word, a dirty look or a slightly careless attitude can be enough to trigger a household tsunami. Like magic, a circumstantial sprain is turned into an insurmountable contortion with the potential to evolve into an emotional fracture!

If splitting wood is a male thing, splitting hairs is a female thing. A situation is turned inside out and overanalyzed from all angles, like the camera tube that performs panoramic dental x-rays. Then, after hours or days of nonstop debate, a verdict is rendered: either there is no problem, or there is one. In the first case, the husband will get out of it with a small penalty. In the second case, an inner turmoil can begin that causes a husband to feel like he's been sent to the electric chair.

The instinctual reaction of a man is invariably to try to calm her down, and say something like: "It will be okay, dear!" Big mistake! As I found when reading *Men Are from Mars and Women Are from Venus*, coddling is the last thing a woman expects from her man. I was blown away by this information. After applying my male reasoning to my own experience and the experience of others, I've seen extremely clear evidence that there are few things in day-to-day life that can't be solved by calmly discussing them.

But a woman relates to this tactic in a different manner: His attempt to calm her down is interpreted as belittling her torment, so the most highly recommended way to react in such a situation is to relate to her anguish. After I'd processed this information for a little while, my wife complained about something. Naturally, my first instinct was to calm her down as I had before: "It's not a big deal. It'll be okay!" But I told myself I should try another approach.

So, I started approving her feelings: "Yes, dear, you're right. It's a delicate situation. I don't know how we're going to solve this!" I was astonished. As I was playing to her mood, I could see how she was magically calming down. The effects of my endeavor were incredible. I do advise you, dear friends, to apply this tactic because its efficiency is extraordinary!

On the other hand, let's all admit it: Many times, a man's indolence is enough to make a saint swear. More than once, women turn their faces up to the sky and mentally shout: "What's going in his mind?" They're frustrated about their husbands' lackadaisical attitudes about the events in their lives. So, why wouldn't they scream? Therefore, solving hardships often falls on wives, and the husbands become nothing more than stooges.

If Archimedes had been married, I'm sure he would have said something like: "Give me a leverage point, and my wife will turn the Earth upside down!"

Even though the paragraphs above may sting, I hope you'll remember that they're soaked in the ink of humor, and will be transformed into delicate caresses. In that train of thought, let me share these wonderful lines from "Song for the Women" by Adrian Paunescu:

> *Men are careless, and women are very calm.*
> *Men mess up what women make clear.*
> *Men only soles, women only hands.*
> *This is a woman's destiny!*
> *With all the steps around the house,*
> *For which they ask no pay,*
> *Had they started off on a glorious path,*
> *They would have reached beyond the sky!*
> *You are the threaded link*
> *In each chain that links the two.*
> *How hard it is to have you, women, in our lives,*
> *But life's impossible without you!"*

The Impossible Dream

Someone once said: "Every woman wants a delicate, attentive, understanding man, who has good communication skills and who is simultaneously strong, harsh and masculine. Unfortunately, she can't have him because he already has a boyfriend!"

Some women hold impossibly high standards for their spouses. Since no heterosexual man in the world exists like the one described above, women who want this kind of husband end up continuously discontented and trip over the dust on the road. Even if they don't trip over it, it will certainly get in their eyes! And if these women get married, their husbands become renewable sources of that dust.

No matter what these husbands do or how much effort they put into something, it's never enough. Did he even bend over backwards to satisfy her? The immediate reply is: "Just once, honey? Why not twice?" Did he pluck the moon from the sky and give it to her? He will hear her sigh: "Oh, how dark it is outside!"

In the end, it's every woman's right to decide what impresses her most about her man: the hairiness that embellishes his strong chest or the heart that beats inside it; the decibels in his voice or the kind words that soothe her soul; the strong arms that can lift a heavy load or the soft hands that can gently caress her. Whatever her preference is, she's perfectly right!

Female readers, I'm going to clearly state this, in order to save you a lot of conflict: In all likelihood, you won't be able your cake and eat it, too! If the man beside you is sensitive to your inner needs and has good communication skills, he's probably not going to be a macho man when you need him to be! It's not in him; he doesn't have that tool in his bag of tricks! And if your man exudes masculinity from every pore, you probably won't find the sensitivity your delicate soul longs for. Admitting this probability will remove a lot of stress from your relationship.

All spouses need to accept that when they get married, they have to make some compromises, at least to some degree. By choosing one person, they are also choosing that person's imperfections. This is one of the fundamental truths in the world, just as day comes after a night or the earth revolves around the sun. To admit this reality equals a huge dose of wisdom and an unbeatable couple!

The Notebook

I recently re-watched the emotional film *The Notebook*. In it, an old man went to a nursing home every day to have breakfast with his wife, who had lived there for years after being diagnosed with Alzheimer's disease. In all those years, he never missed a single morning.

One day, he arrived late and approached the nurses' cabin to ask them if breakfast had been served yet. One of the nurses looked at him and warmly replied: "No, stay calm. Not yet."

The old man exhaled, and the bouquet of flowers he held in his hands seemed to come to life. The nurse continued, Even if you were late, it wouldn't be a tragedy because she doesn't know who you are anyway." The old man looked her straight in her eye and said, "Yes, but I still know who she is..."

I do know who you are, my dearest Gina!

160

Chapter 15: Motherhood

I believe in love at first sight, because I've loved my mother since I opened my eyes.
Anonymous

In one of Ruxandra's homework projects, here's how she described my wife:

"My mother is forty years old. She lives in Sibiu. Her eyes are as brown as wood. Her hair is as black as ebony, and she is of a moderate height. She gives us advice to help us in life. She is loving and friendly, and she loves her family like her angels. She has a passion for reading because she says that books will help one in harsh times. Those around her appreciate her for her wit, intelligence and tidiness. She is a lawyer. I love her with all my heart; she is the most precious being in the world to me."

Excellent Examples

My wife and I love Ruxandra and Georgia with all our hearts. Nevertheless, there are moments when we feel as if we can no longer cope with everything that raising and educating children entails. Then I think about how hard it must have been for my mother to raise two children all by herself in harsher times than today! And she exceled at everything she did. She was completely devoted and sacrificed so much for us.

I can say wholeheartedly that my wife's mother is also an example of involvement, devotion and sacrifice. It is a privilege for us to have two individuals beside us who have given most of their lives to their children! Their example helps us more effectively raise and educate our daughters.

Besides the fact that both my brother and I consider ourselves accomplished individuals, each time I reminisce about my childhood, I enjoy it. Yes, I can say it wholeheartedly: I had a happy childhood!

Mother placed a lot of trust in me, but she also made me accountable for a lot. So if I saw my friends playing with a ball on the way home from school, I would leave my schoolbag in the house and go play without a maternal reprimand! Once the play period ended, I would quietly go back into the house and do my homework.

However, I occasionally revolted against my mother for various reasons, which I considered well-grounded at the time. I told myself I was entitled to reproach her for this or that, and I felt like I needed to put distance between us. Now I regret every second when my soul removed itself from hers out of spite.

We all make mistakes, even mothers. But I think we should turn a blind eye to them, due to their unique roles. *A good mother can take the place of anyone, but no one can replace her!*

Thank you for everything, mother!

Just Passing Through

During natural childbirth, the pain is so intense that a woman can finally understand what a man goes through when he has a cold!

In life, everything passes eventually. But if you're not prioritizing, it can feel like removing a kidney stone. I'm speaking from my own personal experience! Four years ago, I suddenly felt an intense pain in the lumbar region, which turned out to be caused by a stone that began its trip in the kidney and stopped somewhere in my left ureter.

Because of the kidney stone, I suffered for nine months. During this time, I had four episodes of kidney pain. Women who have both given birth and gone through kidney colic say they would prefer the pain of childbirth at any time. As far as I am concerned, I gave birth to a stone!

Atlas was actually a woman

As you can see from Genesis 3:16, women continue to suffer, due to one woman taking a bite from a single apple: "I will greatly multiply your pain in childbirth, in pain you will bring forth children; yet your desire will be for your husband, and he will rule over you."

Dear female readers, this passage explains how you found that the burdens of this world have been handed over to you from generation to generation, and you had no opportunity to oppose it or protest against it!

They say *behind every great man there's an even greater woman. But more often than not, there's no one behind a strong woman!* With that in mind, I'm convinced that the Great Creator also mindfully used certain materials to create the first humans. Could someone made of clay carry burdens, including his own body? No, not a chance!

That's why women had to be built of more resilient material, such as a man's rib. With this sturdiness as a foundation, women are more capable of coping with all the pressures that life throws at them—sometimes with breathtaking force.

So where does this extraordinary force come from? The question is justified, especially since women tend to be so much more beautiful and graceful. I'd say the explanations must be at least twofold:

- The changes that emerge inside a woman after she gives birth to children.
- The genetic difference between a man and a woman which resides in the 23rd pair of chromosomes. Females have two X chromosomes,

and males have an X chromosome and a Y chromosome. Now imagine placing a load on XX, which is supported on four legs that stand in perfect balance. And now envision placing a load on XY—which is fragile from the get-go, since it has three legs. Which load do you think will be better supported?

Remember, a woman is only helpless until her nail polish dries off!

Unenthusiastic Cry

The first cry of a newborn is not enthusiastic. How could you cry out for joy when you've just exited the comfortable and warm bed of the womb? From a medical perspective, it's actually a rather desperate cry. But soon, arms full of emotion and concern envelop the infant. And like magic, he or she calms down and is enveloped in a feeling of safety that assures it that its mother will never abandon it.

Even if a mother cannot hold her children's hands throughout their lives, she will never detach herself from their souls.

Most mother/child bonds could never be severed because they were forged for nine months between two beating hearts—one next to the other. They even nurture each other—one with blood and nourishment, the other with that unique feeling for which, I must admit, I envy all women being able to bear: the feeling of being absolutely needed.

I have no idea what it actually feels like for a mother to see her child for the first time, so I envy all mothers on Earth.

Role Reversal

When thinking about how much gratitude you should have for your mother, don't forget about the reality of being a woman. Consider this story:

"A man was fed up with going to work every day, and his wife staying at home all day long. He wanted to see for himself what was going on in the house while he was working tooth and nail at the office. So he said, 'God, I go to work every day, and I work eight hours a day while my wife stays at home and has no care in the world. I want her to know what I go through on a daily basis. So please allow me to change places with her for one day. Amen!' And God, in His infinite wisdom, fulfilled this wish.

The next morning, the man woke up in his wife's body and took on her role, and he felt pretty confident about it. "She" got up, made breakfast for her "husband," woke up the children, prepared their clothes, served them breakfast, made their lunches, took them to school, quickly came back home, picked up all the clothes and washed them, went to the bank, went shopping for groceries, put the groceries way, and paid the monthly bills.

When "she" came back home, "she" cleaned the cat's litterbox and washed the dog. It was already

166

1:00 in the afternoon. Then "she" made the beds and picked up other clothes, vacuumed and dusted the house, and washed everything in the kitchen. "She" then ran to school to pick up the children, brought them home, made them something to eat, and helped them with their homework. Then "she" set up the ironing board and started ironing clothes.

At 4:30, "she" started peeling potatoes and washing vegetables for dinner. After dinner, "she" cleaned the entire kitchen, picked up clothes, gave the children baths, and got them ready for bed. At 9 o'clock, "she" was already exhausted from all the work "she" had done, but "her" day was not over yet. The "husband" was waiting for "her" in bed to make love, which "she" successfully performed, without complaints from "her" partner.

The next day, the man woke up and immediately fell to his knees, praying: 'God, I don't know what was in my head when I asked you to put me in my wife's shoes. I was wrong to envy her so much, thinking that she was wasting time at home all day long! Please, pretty please, change us back to the way we were! Amen!'

God, in His infinite wisdom, replied, 'Son, I think you have learned an important lesson, and I would gladly change you back. But you see, you'll have to wait nine months. You got pregnant last night, and you're having a baby!' "

Chapter 16: Fatherhood

"On the pathway of my life,
There were thorns, and there were flowers.
Today, my children walk in my footsteps.
But their life is cloudless!"
Classic Romanian Song Lyrics

A few months before my second daughter was born, I started thinking about a solution to a problem that many families experience when expecting a second child: The firstborn gets jealous, since almost all of the parents' attention is now focused on their little sister or brother. Afterward, a myriad of frustrations begins that can become increasingly unacceptable.

After a few days, I came up with an idea that turned out to be brilliant. I showed Ruxandra an image of a vivisected heart on my computer:

"You see, love, this is what my heart looks like. It has four chambers: one for you, one for Georgia, one for Mummy, and one for me. Which one do you want to stay in?"

Of course, she chose the left ventricle, as it's the largest. "Now let me tell you that no one will ever enter your chamber—not Georgia or Mummy, or even me. It's 100% yours. Understand?"

"Yes, Daddy, I understand," she replied.

After three months, I discovered that she really had understood my point when we passed a woman holding a small baby in her arms. I asked Ruxandra:

"After Georgia is born, who will you love the most? Mummy, Daddy, or your little sister?"

Her reply was prompt: "Well, all the same because each you has your own chamber!"

I leaned down and looked her in the eye: "Bravo, Ruxandra, that's it! There are four chambers in your heart: one for Mummy, one for Daddy, one for Georgia, and one for you—because it's very important to love yourself!"

Do you know what my little 7-year-old wonder said to me?

"Yes, Daddy, it's important, but it's more important to love others!"

I think this chamber idea can be successfully used by all parents who have a child that might have a difficult time adjusting to a new sibling. If your family will have three children after the new baby is born, you can simply say that the fourth chamber is reserved for your spouse. If you'll have four children, each will have his or her own chamber. And if you'll have five children, there's no reason to despair since the left atrium has a small additional chamber (an ear-shaped pouch called the left atrial appendage) that's just right for a newborn. But if you have six children, I hope you aren't expecting any ideas from me!

The Parental Mask

I heard a story about a father who was walking along a dirt road with his little girl. At one point, he cautioned her: "Watch your step, dear!" "Don't worry, dad, I'm walking in your footsteps…"

It's human nature for children to trust their parents. Generally, parents are an oasis of peace for their children as they provide the place where they feel safest. Children's smiles are often closely connected to the protection they experience in the presence of their parents.

We are the foundations on which they structure their personalities, the mirrors where they are most frequently see their reflections. So, we are the most important components in their universe. By the time children realize that their role models are tainted by weaknesses and negative traits, we've already inked large parts of our beings on their skin, just like Carla's Dreams.[9] That's why we need to give the best of ourselves to our children because they will be instilled in their souls and spirits. This effort will bear better fruit, which you can enjoy together.

I recently saw a video on Facebook that really demonstrates the value children can put on their parents. In the gym of a school, parents were called in and asked the following question: "If you could have dinner with anyone in this world, who would you choose?" Without exception, their answers involved admirable or intriguing celebrities. Then the video showed these parents' emotional reactions as they watched their children answering the same question. Without exception, their children said they wanted to have dinner with their parents!

Her soul and my back

One of Georgia's favorite places is on my right shoulder. When she says "Daddy, I want your arms," I

---

[9] Carla's Dreams is a Romanian music group who paints their faces.

know that seconds after I pick her up, her right cheek will rest there, sighing in satisfaction. In the last two years, I have had some back problems, which stole some of the moments when I'd get to hold her.

During one of the summer holidays, I sent Georgia to Galati, where she was spoiled by my wife's parents for an entire month. However, she started longing for us, so I went to get her. On the day she knew I was on the road, she couldn't sleep in anticipation of my arrival. The moment I entered the house, her excitement was tangible!

"Georgia, one second as I drop my bags, and then I will take you in my arms," I said.

Her answer instantly melted my heart, "Daddy, doesn't your back hurt any more?"

The Weight of Maturity

They say most women reach full maturity by age 20, but most men don't reach it until 30. But then someone smarter shoves a marriage licence and a picture of his kids in his face, who need him!

Only retain the humor of this statement, and ignore the complete disregard for being the head of the family. Many men don't consider their responsibilities as a husband and a father to be burdens, but signs of their success. The first to come to mind is my godfather, whose picture you can find in the *Romanian Explanatory Dictionary* under the word "worthiness."

Even with the weight fatherhood entails, I think a father's job is easier than a mother's. Often, taking care of the children is mostly incumbent on the mother as if the nine months prior to birth weren't

171

enough! For instance, my father would scurry away to go to work early in the morning. Frequently, he looked relieved, as if he'd been excused from a burden that Hercules couldn't have managed. But then we'd anxiously wait to see him riding back from the factory on his bike, and when he walked in the door, we'd jump on him with the excitement we felt from missing him all day long.

We were annoyed by the rules our mother had to enforce, and we'd noticed long ago that he was far more willing than her to play down to our level and make our lives more colorful as she was already tired of everything involved with maternity.

It must be really frustrating for mothers whose children view their fathers as much more appealing.

The Toothache Test

One day, I went to pick Ruxandra up after school, and when I found her, her chin was shaking. "What happened, love?"

"Daddy, my tooth hurts! It's hurt all day!" By the time we got home, she was in so much pain that tears were rolling off her beautiful cheeks.

I knelt down and said: "Ruxandra, trust daddy. It will be all right!"

I called a dentist who was my colleague at the university. After about an hour, I was holding Ruxandra's hand as we left the dentist's office, full of the satisfaction that all parents have when they solve their children's important problems.

"What did I tell you, love?" I asked. "Trust daddy, and it'll all be OK."

She replied: "Well, I only wanted to test you to see if you can handle it!"

On the car ride back home, I called my mother to tell her the latest news about her granddaughter. Then I passed the phone back to Ruxandra. At one point, I heard her saying: "Yes, grandma, he handled it. You have given birth to a good son!"

Daddy's Girls

When Ruxandra was about three and a half years old, we took her to visit our godchildren. She was playing cops and robbers with Tudor, who was five years old. At one point, he pointed his rifle at me. Very alarmed, Ruxandra proclaimed, "No, please don't shoot daddy. Shoot me!" Her reaction certainly made a lasting impression.

About a year later, we were both in the living room, and I fondly watched her play. At one point, she raised her wonderful four-year-old eyes and met my gaze. "What's going on, Daddy?"

I got close to her and said, "Ruxandra, look into my eyes and tell me, what do you see?"

She looked carefully, and after thinking about it for about two seconds, she said, "I see... an... I love you!"

"Extraordinary, that's exactly what I was thinking!" I excitedly replied.

"But I didn't see any letter!" she said with candor.

Then when I went to pick up Ruxandra after her first day at kindergarten, I kept imagining how she'd react when she saw me. Her reaction was beyond my expectations. She started pointing at me and shouting in delight: "Daddy! Daddy is here! Look, there's my daddy!" And that was not all. The teacher told me she had asked the children to draw anything they pleased, and they all drew trees, flowers, animals and houses—except Ruxandra. She drew her daddy...

Later, Ruxandra was away at her aunt's, and I was talking on the phone. I asked her: "Did you get my text?"

"Yes, Daddy! Dana came and told me I had a message from you. She asked me if I wanted her to read it to me, but I told her I would read it myself because I would read it more lovingly."

And it already looks like Ruxandra won't be the only daddy's girl in the family. Georgia, my youngest daughter, sent me an extremely strong sign about the relationship we'd have later in life. Just after we brought her home from the maternity ward, I was changing her diaper when she suddenly decided that she'd empty her bladder. She was so enthusiastic that she sprayed me from head to toe, even though she was lying on her back!

Upon hearing this story, my friend's inspired reply was: "You know what this means, Dan? She marked her territory!"

No News from the Newlyweds

An old man asked a computer store to repair his phone. "But your phone is all right!" With tears in his eyes, the old man asked, "Then how come my children don't call me anymore?"

It's so easy to forget the individuals who gave us life when we move into our own houses! We choose to focus our energy on our new family, and suddenly we realize we haven't talked to our parents in a while.

I don't think they deserve this kind of an attitude. So let's not forget about those who shall gravitate toward us their entire lifetimes. They don't need much! The wisdom they've acquired over the years tells them to wait patiently backstage for the time when we will call them onstage and perform someday.

They know they're no longer in leading roles, and although they won Oscars in the movies of our early lives, they're pleased to have insignificant roles, just to be close to us. It's usually not a big deal to text them or give them a ring every few days, just to let them know we're thinking about them fondly.

The harsh reality is that love is the only thing of which most people can never get their fill, yet it's the one thing most people are least likely to give to those who are worthiest of it. *If love can't be measured, then we can at least give it without measure!*

A Father's Longing

I have long waited to find a special poem in which the main character is the father...for no other reason than that mothers have received in full their well-deserved share of admiration and gratefulness through the years. In fact, they have been sung about, written about, and celebrated with holidays and dozens and dozens of flowers! And why not dedicate odes to them? Family life gravitates around them, like the earth revolving around the sun.

That's all well and good. But what about the one who has released his creative energies since the conception process, so the little wonders could appear in this world and feel loved and protected?

In this state of mind, my gaze suddenly fell on a wonderful poem by Romanian author Marin Sorescu. I couldn't wait to share it with you:

When our children are small,
We are DADDIES for them,
How delicate and good that sounds:
'DADDY, I MISS YOU!'
But years go by, and suddenly,
You are now a FATHER.
But that also sounds good:
'FATHER, I MISS YOU!'
But they grow, and you're no longer to their liking.

From a father, you become an OLD MAN,
And these words sound sad and empty:
'OLD MAN, give me another penny!'
But life is but a fire of straws.
They will call you just GRANDPA,
And their words stun you:
'GRANDPA, what else do you need?'
Child, know this:
I have been a faithful father
And from the little I had, if I had it,
I put myself aside and gave to you…
But please give me this much:
If you come to me at the cemetery,

Do say it as you did in childhood:
'DADDY, I MISS YOU!'

But I think the poem more accurately reflects what happens to fathers of boys. Some of the phrases are way too harsh to belong to most daughters, whose natural sensitivity usually prevents them from using such words.

Ruxandra was hovering around me when I discovered this piece. As if to tie up my thoughts with a ribbon, she concluded, "I don't like this poem, Daddy! It's too sad, and I don't think it's true. I will always call you only DADDY for my entire life!"

On one of my summer holidays, when Ruxandra was seven, I took her to my wife's grandparents, Silvica and Georgel. Because the distance to Galați was quite long, I agreed to meet Florin, my brother-in-law, who was to meet us half-way and take her the rest of the way. When it was time for her to come back home, we did the same. So, at one point the cars we were stopped at the edge of the road at a distance of a short distance from each other. There followed a scene as if from a movie! The moment I stepped out of the car, the back door of Florin's car opened, and Ruxandra sprinted toward me with open arms and at the speed of light! I leaned over, she jumped into my arms, and I squeezed her tightly to my chest. After a moment, I realized she was crying. She withdrew her head from my shoulder and looked at me in turmoil, warm tears rolling down her cheeks, "Daddy, I'm crying in happiness!"

"I'm not letting you go anymore!"

One of my good friends, whom the walk of life has taken to the U.S., told me how hard it was to have left his home, especially since his little girl, Mary, lived in Romania. He soon realized that it was imperative to make a decision about the path he was going to choose: his career or his little girl.

His most recent trip to the U.S. forced him to stay there for almost a year, so he didn't see her during that time. Returning to Romania, his daughter waited for him at the airport; she was three and a half years old. When Mary saw him, she approached him resolutely, and without saying a word, she took him by the hand, and they stayed that way until they got home. That special moment altered his perspective...and resulted in an important decision.

The Two Wolves

"A member of the Cherokee tribe sat with his son on the edge of a lake and taught him this lesson: 'In each man's life, there is a formidable fight between two wolves. One is bad; it is the epitome of anger, envy, greed, arrogance, fear, slyness, resentment and self-pity. The other one is good; it brings joy, peace, humbleness, trust, generosity, truth and pity.'

'Which one will win?' the son asked.

'The one you feed...' "

Let us help our children feed the mouths of goodness and beauty within them. Then they can be prepared for the road ahead, as well as the obstacles they meet on that road. It is essential to teach them "to be," since life will prepare them for "to have." The moment when they "will be," they acquire something that no one can take away from them!

So let's be the good parents we always wanted to have. Good parents give their children roots so deep they'll never forget where their home is, yet they endow them with wings to fly to a place where they can show what they've learned from their parents.

Chapter 17: Communication

"God keeps you safe from hands that once applauded you!"
Romanian Expression

We have all seen people lose their way as they were travelling beside us. They are people in whom we have invested our trust, confessed our thoughts and shared emotions that we haven't shared with anyone else. Well, some friends leave us with the certainty that our secrets will be safe with them. That's because they're upstanding people who know how to keep secrets.

But as the quote above implies, there are some friends (or frenemies) who show their true colors after you part ways, proving that their set of values is afflicted by osteoporosis. These are people who think that a true friend cannot be bought, but he can be sold! If you discover that you have this kind of friend, I advise you not to take it personally. Just keep your distance, but maintain the appearance of friendship because they know too much about you to make them your enemy.

Traffic Signs

We are all a sum total of lights and shadows. It's only natural to keep our less honorable thoughts and deeds in the dark. We all have pages of our lives that we hope don't get published. Some people who once applauded us now use their hands to slap us in the face, exposing us to the world and gaining satisfaction from it. They purposefully forget all the good we once did for them. *And those who forget aren't worth it...*

They say people are like traffic signs: Some deserve a priority (like express lanes), and others should be avoided (like No Parking signs). And still others are really worth halting for (like stop signs).

If we continued our journey through life without some friends, it was due to an emotional fracture. Unlike bone fractures, emotional fractures invariably result in vicious calluses. Yes, a broken connection can be restored. Those who have wronged us can catch up with us, but will they walk beside us with a smile as warm as before? I doubt it! As Nicolae Iorga once said, *"The hardest thing in life is not to forgive, but to put your faith in someone again..."*

A Kiss on the Cheek

If I come back from a holiday, and there are four female young doctors/practitioners in the doctors' lounge, I would enthusiastically say hello to them, and I might even give them a platonic kiss on the cheek in greeting. So, if a nurse comes into the room the moment I enter the resident's intimate space (the 45 cm around her) to place an absolutely innocent kiss on her cheek, she won't view it suspiciously since there are three other people in the room.

However, if you move that same scenario to a private office and remove the other three people, the nurse would probably at least question it after she closes the door. The worst-case scenario would involve heated gossip and rumors. Therefore, bear in mind what I say: everything you do in public cannot be misinterpreted!

Reflexive Thunder

Consider this scenario: You're in heavy traffic, and the driver in front of you turns on his right turn signal. You start to pass them, and to your dismay, you realize the driver is actually turning left! A collision is imminent, but you have good reflexes and manage to avoid it. You both pull over, and you angrily get out of the car and go straight over to the guilty driver to "caress" his ear drums with all the words you've been holding in.

But as the warm and grateful driver gets out of his car, the entire avalanche of invectives magically melts: Your boss, an extremely kind person, has just bought a new car, and still isn't familiar with all the features. It's good that you didn't thunder against him in a proletarian rage and self-righteously proclaim that you never would have done what he just did.

I Ran or Iraq

Now think about a person you find to be unpleasant. You'd rather cross the street than see the color of this person's eyes. But if you suddenly see that same person you dislike in Iraq after spending the last six months there, don't tell me you'd at least have the urge to say hello, if not start a conversation with them!

The Nausea of Conflict

Under the circumstances of diverse opinions and characters, the incongruence between them cannot be solved by using the mind's logical and cold reasoning but by using the warm understanding that derives from the kindness of the soul.

If we make a small analysis, the number of disputes whose origin resides in trifles is higher than the number of disputes caused by moments that truly matter in our lives. In the end, it's only natural: You cannot experience an important event each and every day. The outcome of circumstances bearing the potential to develop a dispute depends on how much we are willing to take in, and more importantly, how we metabolize our interlocutor's ideas. If the "feast" takes place in the "cold attic" of the brain, we will often suffer from "indigestion" as a result of the ways others' ideas and beliefs are served to us.

If they aren't among our favorite "dishes," a nauseating effect will occur that sits heavily on the stomach, stimulating the gallbladder to produce more bile. But if such a discussion takes place like a picnic on the green grass of the soul, bathed in the warm rays of kindness, we would all be able to enjoy the food. Then our conclusions could be naturally absorbed as nurturing principles that will contribute to our development as human beings.

The Power of Words

I saw a short video entitled *The Power of Words* on Facebook.[10] A beggar on the street had a small jar for money and a cardboard sign that said, "I'm blind. Please help." Every so often, some people passing by would take pity on him and throw him a

---

[10]https://www.youtube.com/watch?v=CNhYbJbqg-Y

183

coin. At one point, a young woman approached, put a banknote in his jar, and left. She took a few steps, stopped, pondered for a second, and turned back. She leaned over, took the cardboard, and started writing on the back.

Meanwhile, the beggar, not knowing what was going on, felt her shoes so he would be able to recognize her if she reappeared. The young woman placed the cardboard near the beggar, walked away, and was soon lost in the crowd.

Soon, people passing by the beggar read the writing on the cardboard and repeatedly gave him money. After a while, the young woman returned and stopped in front of the beggar, looking pleased at the jar full of coins. The beggar touched her shoes, recognized them, and asked, "What did you do to my sign?"

She smiled and replied, "I wrote the same thing, but with different words."

Here's what she wrote: "It's a beautiful day, and I can't see it!"

Words are powerful! Aldous Huxley compared them to X-rays: If used as they should be, words can pass through anything. Even Dumbledore agreed with him the last *Harry Potter* book: "Words are, in my not-so-humble opinion, our most inexhaustible source of magic, capable of both inflicting injury and remedying it." The more they're loaded with genuine emotion, the more impact they have. I personally prefer a warm yet silent soul to a cold soul that produces heartless words.

Sweet Poison

Many problems in our lives would disappear if we talked to each other directly, instead of behind each other's back!

Gossip is sweet poison dripped in the ears of those around us, which leaks straight into the soul of the one who's spreading it, nurturing the pettiness inside with flavor and converting them, for a moment, into some sort of a hero whose verbal spit is sipped by a member of the public who's willing to disparage someone. If you are in such an entourage, of course you cannot always make a gossiper shut up, but you can choose whom you lend your ears to. After a prior sudden spin on your heel, your movement from a backbiter's operating range will be an indicative of how willing you are to appreciate the elegance of their speech.

It's much easier to demolish than to build, to blame than to bless, to throw mud instead of flowers. Especially if discrediting someone will create a benefit for us, someone will always take satisfaction from participating in innocent gossip. But there is no such thing! One can never foresee the effect that any kind of gossip can have on its target. In fact, "innocent" gossip can make a mountain out of a molehill, so its impact could be devastating.

God created us without shame. Sinning has darkened the brilliance His breath bestowed onto us. Instead of bringing forth the little good that still flickers in us to light, so we can enjoy its beauty, we'd rather cover it in the black soot of gossip. We often partake in this endeavor with toxic satisfaction, without realizing that we actually build the scaffolding of our future blame.

The Magnificent Pearl

Romanian philosopher Gabriel Liiceanu once said: "It is very easy to hurt someone's soul because the soul walks barefoot, and its footsteps pick up all the thorns in a day." These great words are full of sensitivity and packed with truth. They say that ten phrases that insult your intelligence can be passed over much easier than one phrase that assaults your soul. If the energy a heart releases is 500 times greater than the one issued by the brain, well, its sensitivity is that much greater! Any negative disruption of the energy field is experienced in full!

Many times, a soul's receptors are so sensitive that we find ourselves under the weather and don't know why. Most of the time, we have to retrospectively look back at the events we've been through, the people we've encountered, and the replies we've received to identify the reason for our bad attitude. However, the cause sometimes remains somewhere in the dark.

No matter how much we train ourselves to stand against the inherent aggressions we experience throughout life, we can never avoid suffering. Specifically, the soul doesn't always have the same power. Yesterday, it went quite easily through a trial, but the blow of today will sensitize it enough that an attack will not be so easily parried as it would be tomorrow. Once the shield is penetrated, negative energies that would have otherwise bashed into it will easily creep into the soul, creating a wild stomp that will shake it to its roots!

Anybody can bring the dirt inside a man out to the surface, but there are few who prefer to dig up the gold in a man. So let us care for the treasure buried inside ourselves and in those around us. Regardless of how sophisticated or rudimentary they appear to us, let's cherish them!

Some people are like clams found at the bottom of the sea: They're simple, but their souls are like magnificent pearls waiting to be discovered.

Precarious Honesty

Everyone appreciates honesty until you're completely honest with them about something they don't want to hear. Then, they say you are a jerk!

Isn't this truism frustrating? It doesn't matter how many good things you've done for that person. It doesn't matter that you spoiled them with your attention, or that they could count on you during hard times. If you offend them by being too frank, they suddenly become stricken with amnesia about the good things you showered on them, and they only remember that you hurt their pride.

Someone once said that people trip over the truth, but they usually get back on their feet and move on. However, now they'll be walking with a limp, which they'll obviously blame on you. Since the Paleolithic era, men have carved bad news in stone, but they scrawl good news in the sand! Therefore, an overly honest approach is the shortest distance between two troubles.

There are truths that put you down, and there are lies that lift you up. As Tudor Gheorghe sang, "Life without lies would not be a paradise!" So my advice is to let the little shortcomings of those around you pass, so you can enjoy their great qualities.

Alternatively, *you can feel free to always speak the truth. Then run...*

Socrates' Three Filters

In situations when we encounter gossip, we need to use the Three Filters that Socrates proposed. Once day, the philosopher saw an acquaintance running toward him, shouting, "Socrates, do you have any idea what I've just heard about one of your students?"

"Before you tell me," Socrates interrupted, "Please answer these three questions, so we can test what you intend to share with me. The first is the Test of Truth. Are you absolutely sure that what you want to tell me is true?"

"No," the man replied. "In fact, I just heard—"

"It's all right," Socrates interrupted again. "So you don't actually know if it's true or not. Now let's try the second test, which is the Test of Goodness. Is this information about my student good?"

"No, on the contrary—"

"So you want to tell me something bad about him, and you aren't sure if it's true?"

The man raised his shoulders, a little embarrassed. Socrates continued.

"You can still pass the trial, because the Test of Utility remains. Is this information useful to me?"

"No, not really..."

Socrates concluded, "If what you want to tell me isn't true, good, or even useful, then why say it at all?"

You can find out more about a person from how they speak about others than from what others say about them. Brilliant minds discuss ideas, but small minds discuss other people. Mediocre individuals can be easily identified: They do not appreciate, approve or encourage. They just querulously condemn and create conflict!

For some time, I have personally striven to consistently apply Socrates' filters, as I've found I get quite consumed by people bringing varied—yet essentially nasty—comments to my attention. Eventually, each of us will make an inappropriate remark about someone around us, so a certain muddy word is taken out of context and blown out of proportion. In such situations, I believe that self-imposed ignorance can bring us more benefits. At a psychological level, *what you don't know can't hurt you!* Moreover, if someone talks behind your back, it means they aren't brave enough to say it to your face, so they aren't worth banging your head against a wall.

My dears, the world is already full of querulous, gossipy, stiff and uncaring people. So there's no need to increase their numbers!

Conclusions

"To know even one life has breathed easier because you have lived. This is to have succeeded."
Ralph Waldo Emerson

Here are the two most important takeaways from this book:

1. Heaven Is Within. It's available to each of us. God took the time to give each of us this extraordinary opportunity.
2. The easiest way to discover the Kingdom of God is by interacting with people around us.

Almost everything is up to us: What's actually happening makes up 10% of the outcome, and the way we react is 90%.

To begin, we have to try to refrain from judging others. Any person could be like Teddy Stallard, who carries inner burdens we're not aware of.

And let's not forget that every blow we receive has two cures: time and silence. Every wound can be healed. The Great Healer has built a strong foundation inside us, which we can always rest on. So we have all the reasons to maintain an optimistic attitude, and the energy we emanate must be positive. It's vital to act with empathy and generosity toward our fellow men.

To find and keep Heaven Within us, we need to constantly progress. To fulfil our missions in life, we must consistently prioritize and act with compassion.

And our mission is sometimes easier than we could imagine. Just refer to the quote above.

Of course, to achieve this goal, we need balance and integrity. There is no other way. And yes, we often need wisdom to overcome some shortcomings and cure lifelong regrets.

All these dimensions of our personalities can invariably get tested by our fellows. We can polish these qualities that guide us to Heaven Within by interacting with our children, friends, loved ones and partners, but it requires constantly improving our communication skills.

Each stage in life has its own temptations and concerns. For various reasons, we may not be able to juggle everything that comes our way, so we have to prioritize the moments that require us to muster all of our energy, such as experiencing the birth of a child, taking an important exam, or simply working hard at our jobs.

Time marches on, and it numbs the impulses that trigger the physical or spiritual contractions that lead us to fulfilling our desires and aspirations. Naturally, the consequence is physical or spiritual atrophy, which can halt the dreams we once had.

Let's get real: It's impossible to give 100% of ourselves to all of life's circumstances, especially since the natural tendency of our spirit is to seek convenience. Bad habits are like comfortable beds: easy to climb into it, but hard to get out of. In addition, the persistence of an unhealthy habit can eventually lead to serious consequences. Have you ever heard Venus de Milo's excuse for missing her arms? "I started by biting my fingernails..."

We will all die someday, but in the meantime, we have the opportunity to live every day! So let's stop focusing on the black dot, and discover the piece of heaven that resides in each of us. Let's live life to its fullest!

Find HEAVEN WITHIN YOU!